Birnbaum's

Walt Disney World FOR KIDS BY KIDS

Jill Safro
Editor

Todd Sebastian Williams
Art Director

Suzy Goytizolo
Associate Editor

Donna McCray-Reid
Copy Editor

Hilary Feldstein
Editorial Assistant

Alexandra Mayes Birnbaum
Consulting Editor

THE OFFICIAL GUIDE

HYPERION AND HEARST BUSINESS PUBLISHING, INC.

ISBN: 0-7868-8481-9

Printed in the United States of America

An enormous debt of gratitude is owed to Kevin Banks, Sheila Butler,
Laura Simpson, Darlene Papalini, Ken Potrock, Gene Duncan, Tim Lewis, Sharon Breger,
Tim Hahn, Karen Granik, and Miriam Levin, all of whom performed above and beyond the
call of duty to make the creation of this book possible. To Phil Lengyel, Tom Elrod, Linda
Warren, Bob Miller, and Charlie Ridgway, thank you for believing in this project in the first
place. And to Wendy Lefkon, special thanks for taking it from idea to reality.

We'd also like to tip our hats to Tom Passavant, editorial director, and to Sue Irsfeld,
proofreader extraordinaire.

Other 2000 Birnbaum's Official Disney Guides

Disneyland
Walt Disney World
Walt Disney World Without Kids

CONTENTS

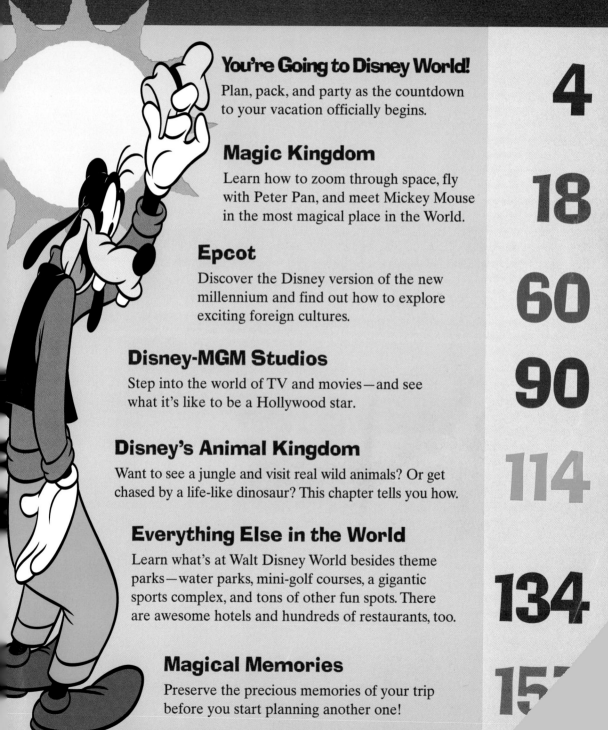

When you first heard the news, you couldn't believe your own ears. Could it be true? Were you really going on a vacation to Walt Disney World? Well, believe it or not, it's true! Before you know it, you'll be in the sunny state of Florida. It's the home of Walt Disney World and the most famous mouse on planet Earth. (Hint: His name starts with "M.")

If you have ever been there, you already know that it's one mighty big place with lots to do. And this year there's more to do than ever before—Walt Disney World is throwing a big party to celebrate the beginning of a new millennium. (You can read all about it on page 12.) In fact, there is so much going on that it can get a little confusing. That's where this book comes in handy. It describes everything in the World, from the Magic Kingdom theme park to the Hoop-Dee-Doo Musical Revue. And it's filled with advice from kids like you.

Disney World!

There is no right or wrong way to read this book. You can start on the first page and read straight through to the end. Or you can skip around, read your favorite parts first, and come back to the rest later.

No matter what you do, one thing is for sure: When you're done, you will be a true-blue Disney expert. Soon kids may start asking you for advice on how to have the most awesome vacation in the World!

Pack a Pencil

Don't leave this book behind when you head for the parks. It's full of tips and opinions that you'll want to remember. There are games and activities, too. So don't forget to bring a pen or pencil.

Play Detective

Sometimes waiting in line for a ride can seem to take forever. To make the time go faster, try to spot all of the objects hidden in Birnbaum's **line games** scavenger hunt. Every time you see Goofy on the lookout, there will be a clue to lead you on your way. Happy hunting!

LINE GAMES

Track Your Trip

Each time you check out an attraction, check it off in this book. Then you'll know what's left to see on your next visit.

Page 160 is an autograph page. Ask Disney characters to sign it!

Search for Hidden Mickeys

Disney Imagineers have hidden images of Mickey all over Walt Disney World. (Many look like the three connected circles that form Mickey's head.) You might see them in shadows, lights, drawings, or even in the clouds at some attractions. Look in this book for red Mickey heads (🔴) to find Hidden Mickey clues.

Keep track of the number of Hidden Mickeys that you discover. That way when the trip is over you can record your findings on the last page of this book's Magical Memories section.

We're Warning You!

Disney rides are full of surprises. That's part of what makes them so much fun. But not everyone likes surprises. So if things like loud noises or fast turns scare you, look at the book's **attraction reaction** warnings before you go on each ride. That way the only surprises you come across will be good ones!

WET
Attraction Reaction

ROUGH

DARK
Attraction Reaction

SCARY
Attraction Reaction

LOUD
Attraction Reaction

What do YOU think?

Do you agree or disagree with any of the kids in this book? Let us know. Keep track of your thoughts in a diary about your Walt Disney World trip. When you get back, send your opinions and "hot tips" in a letter to the editors at:

Walt Disney World For Kids, By Kids 2000
1790 Broadway, 6th Floor
New York, NY 10019

They will read every letter before they write next year's book.

These are the big kids who had a great time helping to put this book together (from left to right: Todd, Jill, and Suzy).

Meet the Experts

Eric, David, Grace, and Jennifer (from left to right) had a blast working on this book!

It's a lot of fun to work on a book like *Walt Disney World For Kids, By Kids*. But it's also a lot of hard work. Every year, a group of kids goes to Walt Disney World with the editors of *Birnbaum's Walt Disney World*. They spend days riding attractions, splashing in pools, and chomping on delicious munchies. (That's

Eric Levin

Eric lives in Fair Lawn, New Jersey. He was 9 years old when he worked on this book. He loves reading and surfing the Internet. When he grows up, he wants to be the transportation director for Walt Disney World. His favorite Disney ride is the Tomorrowland Transit Authority.

David Granik

David lives in New Rochelle, New York. He was 11 years old when he worked on this book. He loves to play baseball and go swimming. He also likes to spend time hanging out with his friends. His favorite Disney ride is Splash Mountain.

Grace Hahn

Grace lives in Bardstown, Kentucky. She was 12 years old when she worked on this book. She loves softball and plays on her school team. She also enjoys playing the clarinet and the piano. Her favorite Disney ride is the Carousel of Progress.

Jennifer Breger

Jennifer lives in Calabasas, California. She was 12 years old when she worked on this book. She enjoys swimming and playing tennis. She also likes to cook and play the alto saxophone. Her favorite Disney ride is Countdown to Extinction.

the fun part.) After each attraction, the kids take notes about their experience in their Disney journals. (That's the work part.) They write about everything they did and saw. What's cool? What's not? Who chickened out at Space Mountain? The kids also try out all of the new activities and games. This book could not have been written without them.

A new group of kids works on this book each year. Who are these kids and where do they come from? You can read about them above and in the pages that follow. The information will give you an idea of whose opinions might be like your own. Their words—along with other descriptions in the book—may help you decide which attractions you just have to see and which you'd like to skip.

HAVE A GREAT TRIP!

Justin Berfield, 1995

Justin lives in Oak Park, California. He was 8 years old when he worked on this book. Justin is an actor, and has been in many movies. He loves animals and has some unusual pets.

Robert Raack, 1994

Robert lives in Eugene, Oregon. He was 8 years old when he worked on this book. Robert is very interested in dragons. He likes to play video games and soccer.

Szasha Ozard, 1998

Szasha (pronounced *SAH-sha*) lives in Petrolia, California. She was 8 years old when she worked on this book. She likes bike riding, fishing, and hiking. She also enjoys sewing.

Lindsay Compton, 1995 & '96

Lindsay lives in Dallas, Texas. She was 9 the first year she worked on this book. She likes to play soccer and basketball. She loves to draw and wants to be an animal doctor someday.

Emma Peters-Axtell, 1997

Emma lives in Duluth, Minnesota. She was 9 years old when she worked on this book. She was on the editorial board of a magazine for kids. She loves to sing and dance.

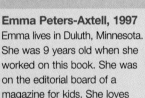

Taran Noah Smith, 1994

Taran lives in San Rafael, California. He was 9 years old when he worked on this book. He's an actor who was Mark on *Home Improvement*. He likes to sail and ride his mountain bike.

Kirsti Harju, 1999

Kirsti lives in Somerset, New Jersey. She was 9 years old when she worked on this book. Kirsti loves kickball, basketball, and bike riding. She has two cats and a fish.

Bradley Sanchez, 1995

Bradley lives in Independence, Missouri. He was 10 years old when he worked on this book. He likes to play football and is a fan of the Kansas City Chiefs. He enjoys playing video games.

Brian Foster, 1997

Brian lives in Woodinville, Washington. He was 10 years old when he worked on this book. He enjoys all kinds of sports. He also likes to work on computers and collect coins.

Robbie Pimentel, 1999

Robbie lives in Richmond Hill, New York. He was 10 years old when he worked on this book. He loves computers and even has his own website. He also likes video games and hockey.

Seth Reuter, 1999

Seth lives in Boca Raton, Florida. He was 10 years old when he worked on this book. He's interested in karate and paleontology. Some day he wants to work for NASA.

Dan Marchand, 1998

Dan lives in Clifton Park, New York. He was 10 years old when he worked on this book. His favorite hobbies are playing video games and all kinds of sports. He also plays the viola.

Michael Howard, 1998

Michael lives in San Antonio, Texas. He was 11 years old when he worked on this book. He enjoys playing basketball and football. He also loves to He has two sisters.

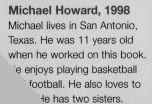

Ashley Pletz, 1994

Ashley lives in Chicago, Illinois. She was 11 years old when she worked on this book. She loves to write. She also takes ballet lessons.

Danielle Gould, 1995
Danielle lives in Potomac, Maryland. She was 11 years old when she worked on this book. Danielle enjoys reading and loves to dance. She takes ballet, jazz, and tap lessons.

Dawna Boone, 1995 & '96
Dawna lives in Natick, Massachusetts. She was 11 the first year she worked on this book. She loves to read and listen to music. She also plays the saxophone.

Lissy Woodhams, 1994
Lissy lives in Tucson, Arizona. She was 11 years old when she worked on this book. She plays the piano, is a member of a drama club, and enjoys horseback riding.

Brian Levinthal, 1994
Brian lives in Huntington, New York. He was 12 years old when he worked on this book. He likes to draw cartoons and play the clarinet. He also likes to swim.

Ashley Johnson, 1997
Ashley lives in Burbank, California. She was 12 years old when she worked on this book. Ashley is an actress who has been on TV shows, including *Growing Pains*.

Adam Farkas, 1997
Adam lives in Miami Beach, Florida. He was 12 years old when he worked on this book. His favorite sports are hockey and football. He also enjoys rock climbing and waterskiing.

Danielle Thomas, 1998
Danielle lives in Danville, Kentucky. She was 12 years old when she worked on this book. She enjoys church activities and going to school. She also plays the saxophone.

Anna Kerlek, 1995
Anna lives in Chagrin Falls, Ohio. She was 13 years old when she worked on this book. She's on her school volleyball, basketball, and track teams. She loves to sing and play the piano.

Tate Lynche, 1995 & '96
Tate lives in St. Petersburg, Florida. He was 13 the first year he worked on this book. He was a Mouseketeer on the *Mickey Mouse Club* show. He enjoys in-line skating.

Amy Newcomer, 1999
Amy lives in Paupack, Pennsylvania. She was 13 years old when she worked on this book. She loves to shop. She also enjoys skiing and playing field hockey.

David Bickel, 1994
David lives in Columbus, Ohio. He was 13 years old when he worked on this book. He is a sports fan who likes the Atlanta Braves and Chicago Bulls. He plays baseball and video games.

Karyn Williams, 1994 & '96
Karyn lives in Orlando, Florida. She was 13 the first year she worked on this book. She is an aspiring actress. She also loves to travel, and once studied marine biology in Australia.

Adam Winchester, 1995
Adam lives in Colorado Springs, Colorado. He was 14 years old when he worked on this book. He loves hockey, basketball, baseball, and soccer. Someday he wants to be an architect.

Nita Booth, 1994
Nita lives in Chesapeake, Virginia. She was 14 years old when she worked on this book. Nita was a Mouseketeer on the *Mickey Mouse Club* show. S loves to sing in her churc

What a Wonderful World

Walt Disney loved dreaming up stories to tell and new ways to tell them. After he died, his brother, Roy, kept one of his biggest dreams alive. He made sure Walt's special "world" was built just the way Walt had imagined it. Roy even insisted that it be called *Walt* Disney World, so everyone would know it was his brother's dream.

Walt Disney World officially opened on October 1, 1971. Since then, millions of people have stopped in for a visit. Some people come to Walt Disney World for a day, but most stay a little longer. There's just so much to see and do.

Pick a theme park, any theme park

The most famous part of Walt Disney World is the **Magic Kingdom**. It's home to Cinderella Castle, Space Mountain, and those rascally Pirates of the Caribbean. It's also where Mickey, Minnie, and their pals keep their country cottages. Kids of all ages can't get enough of this happy place. Of course, there are three other theme parks to see.

 **Epcot** is a wonderland of science and discovery. It's also a great place to take a "world tour." Lots of different countries have shops, restaurants, and attractions inside the theme park. Epcot opened in 1982. You weren't even born yet!

Are you a major movie fan? If so, you'll get a big kick out of the **Disney-MGM Studios** theme park. It's jam-packed with movie-themed rides and exhibits. The secrets of animation are revealed at The Magic of Disney Animation. Belle and Gaston sing their hearts out at Beauty and the Beast Live on Stage. And The Twilight Zone Tower of Terror scares *everybody* silly. The Disney-MGM Studios opened in 1989. How old were you then?

Disney's Animal Kingdom is the newest theme park at Walt Disney World. (It got off to a *roaring* start in 1998.) It has what it takes to make any kid's day: an African safari ride filled with wild animals, life-like dinosaurs, and a super slimy 3-D movie about bugs.

Chill out!

Need to cool off on a hot day? You can make a splash at a Disney water park. Between **River Country**, **Typhoon Lagoon**, and **Blizzard Beach**, it's almost impossible to stay dry. Each one has slippery slides, tube rides, and some very cool pools.

But wait—there's more! Walt Disney World also has boats, bikes, and even horses to ride. It has hundreds of restaurants, shops, and other places to explore. In fact, no matter how many times you visit, there's always something new to see. Will Walt Disney World ever be finished? Not as long as there is imagination left in the world. That's exactly how Walt would have wanted it.

Magical Milestones

Big things are always happening in Disney's world. Here are a few of the greatest moments:

1901 — Walt Disney is born on December 5th, in Chicago, Illinois

1928 — Walt creates Mickey Mouse. Mickey stars in his first movie, *Steamboat Willie*

1937 — Walt's animators finish *Snow White and the Seven Dwarfs*, the first full-length animated movie

1955 — Walt's dream to make a family theme park comes true. Disneyland opens in Anaheim, Califomia

1971 — Walt Disney World (WDW) opens in Orlando, Florida

1975 — Space Mountain, the first WDW roller coaster, opens

1982 — Epcot opens at WDW

1983 — Tokyo Disneyland opens in the capital city of Japan

1987 — The first Disney Store has its grand opening in Glendale, California

1989 — Disney-MGM Studios opens at WDW

1992 — Disneyland Paris opens in France

1997 — WDW celebrates its 25th anniversary

1998 — Disney's Animal Kingdom opens at WDW

2000 — Disney's Millennium Celebration takes over WDW! (Read all about it on the next page.)

Disney's Millennium Celebration

This year the world is celebrating something very big—the beginning of a new millennium! (A millennium is a period of a thousand years.) A major event like that deserves a big party. So Walt Disney World is throwing one, and everybody is invited. How do you prepare for a party like that? By planning activities and doing a lot of decorating. And that's exactly what Disney did.

Take one look at Epcot's Spaceship Earth and you know it's time to celebrate. There's a giant Mickey hand and a magic wand beside it! Disney's Millennium Celebration takes place in Epcot because it's a theme park about discovery. Read on to discover lots of ways to have fun here during the party!

Epcot is the place to be

At first the **Leave a Legacy** sculptures in front of Spaceship Earth look like long, flat walls. But take a closer look. What do you see? Tiny faces all over them. The faces are actually portraits of some of the people who have visited Epcot. (It costs $35 to have your picture added to the wall.) The sculptures are going to stay up long after the Millennium Celebration is over. So years from now you can come back and see how you looked in the year 2000!

Have you ever watched the Olympics on TV? If you have, you might know about **Pin Trading** already. At Walt Disney World it works like this: First you buy some pins (or bring them from home). Then you trade your pins with other guests or cast members. It's a fun way to meet new people and collect some cool souvenirs from all over the world! There are special areas set up at Epcot just for pin trading. The biggest one is called **Millennium Central** in Future World. (You can trade pins in other parts of Walt Disney World, too.) How many different pins can you collect?

There's a whole new pavilion in World Showcase, and it's called **Millennium Village**. Countries from all over the world have brought exhibits to it. Here you can learn what it's like to live in each country. The cast members are from different countries, too. Listen to their stories about their homelands. Then maybe you can teach them something about your country!

Do you like to dance? If so, Epcot has a festival for you! It weaves its way into World Showcase twice a night. The **Tapestry of Nations** is not like most Walt Disney World shows. In this show, Disney characters aren't the stars— *you* are. You're invited to dance, sing, and play musical instruments with gigantic puppets and performers wearing colorful masks and costumes. (To make your own musical instruments for the festival, head to one of the Kidcot Funstops in World Showcase. The instruments are free and they make great souvenirs!) The host of Tapestry of Nations is a tall puppet called the Sage of Time. He welcomes guests and starts the show. Stand in Norway, Morocco, or Canada for the best view.

The big bang!
One of the best parts of the Millennium Celebration comes at the end of the day. It's called **IllumiNations 2000—Reflections of Earth** and it's one hot show! It tells the story of how our planet may have been formed. The show begins with a fiery explosion over the World Showcase Lagoon. Soon you see a huge sphere move across the water and into the center of the lagoon. (The sphere represents the earth.) You can actually see continents forming on it, while dramatic music plays. The planet starts to spin until finally it splits open and a gigantic torch rises out of it. Beautiful fireworks shoot out from the top of the torch and light up Epcot's sky.

HOT TIP

Innoventions, Spaceship Earth, and Millennium Central open at 8:30 A.M.

Getting Ready to Go

P lanning a vacation to Walt Disney World is
lots of fun. But it's not as easy as
it sounds. There are so many
choices to make! Which parks should you
visit? What should you pack? And where can
you meet your favorite Disney characters?
Use this book to answer these questions and
help plan your family's vacation. Remember:
It's never too early to get started!

Make a Simple Schedule

D id you know that there are more than 300 attractions at Walt Disney
World? It could take weeks to see them all. And most people don't
have weeks to spend on vacation! That's why it's important to make a
schedule before you leave home. Without it, you might miss some of the rides
you want to try the most.

What You'll Need
●Paper ●Pencil ●This book

What To Do

1. Write "Magic Kingdom" on the top of a piece of paper.

2. Look at the Magic Kingdom chapter. Every time you see
an attraction that seems like fun, write its name on the paper.

3. When you have finished the chapter, look over your list. Then put
a star next to your ten favorite Magic Kingdom attractions.

4. Now make a schedule for each of the other theme parks you plan to visit.

5. Don't forget to bring your simple schedules to the parks!

Learn the Disney Lingo

Audio-Animatronics: Life-like robots, from birds and dinosaurs to movie stars and presidents. They seem real—but they're not.

Cast Member: A Disney employee.

Circle-Vision 360: A movie that surrounds you. The screens form a circle.

Guidemap: A theme park map that also describes attractions, shops, restaurants, and entertainment.

Imagineer: A creative person who designs Disney theme park attractions.

Save Room for Souvenirs

When you pack for your trip, make sure you're prepared for the weather. Believe it or not, it gets chilly in Florida, especially in the winter. But during the summer it's sizzling hot! It's usually warm during the rest of the year. Layers are a good idea, so you can take something off if you get hot. Remember to pack clothes and shoes that are lightweight and comfortable—since you'll do a lot of walking at the parks. And don't overstuff your suitcase. You'll need room for all the goodies you get at Walt Disney World.

What else should you bring? That's up to you! Here's a short list to help you get started:

- **A sweatshirt or sweater**
- **Broken-in sneakers or shoes**
- **Shorts and pants**
- **Long-sleeved and short-sleeved shirts**
- **A bathing suit**
- **A hat and sunglasses**
- **Sunscreen**

Visit Disney on the Internet

This book is chock-full of information about Disney, but there is another great place to learn about Walt Disney World: the Internet. Visit Walt Disney World's website at *www.disneyworld.com.*

If you have a question, send an e-mail and you will get an answer in a few days. If you have a question and don't have access to the Internet, write to:

Walt Disney World
Box 10000
Lake Buena Vista, FL 32830

COUNTDOWN TO WALT DISNEY WORLD

10 DAYS TILL DISNEY

Make invitations for a special Disney breakfast. Deliver one to everyone in your house.

9

Who lives in this castle?
- (a) Mickey Mouse
- (b) Cinderella
- (c) Sleeping Beauty

Did you finish your Magic Kingdom Simple Schedule?

6

This is a picture of:
- (a) The Tree of Life
- (b) The Swiss Family Treehouse
- (c) A bonsai tree in Japan

Time to finish that Disney-MGM Studios Simple Schedule...

5 MORE DAYS

Get ready for your Disney breakfast! Ask a parent to make Mickey pancakes by connecting three round pancakes on the griddle. Cut out Mickey-shaped confetti to decorate the table.

2 DAYS TO GO!

You won't see any Lion King characters in:
- (a) The Circle of Life
- (b) The Tiki Room
- (c) The Jungle Cruise

Don't forget to finish your Animal Kingdom Simple Schedule!

1 DAY LEFT

Better set your alarm—tomorrow is the big day!

Take a look at a calendar. On which day does your Walt Disney World vacation begin? Once you find it, count back ten days—that's the day you can start this special countdown.

To do it, simply color in the number for each day as it arrives. Then try the daily activity. You can make up your own special activities, too!

8 DAYS LEFT

Make a list with the address of everyone you want to send a postcard to.

7

Which one of these looks the least like a real mountain?

(a) Splash Mountain
(b) Big Thunder Mountain
(c) Space Mountain

Better finish your Epcot Simple Schedule!

4 DAYS

Start Packing!
(Don't forget the sunscreen.)

3

Pick the best ride to go on first in each theme park:

Magic Kingdom:

Epcot:

Disney-MGM Studios:

Animal Kingdom:

Today's the day:

05/19/00

MONTH/DAY/YEAR

You're going to Walt Disney World!

Magic Kingdom

When most people hear the words Walt Disney World, they think of Cinderella Castle, Space Mountain, and, of course, Mickey Mouse. They are all here in the Magic Kingdom, along with much more. That's why so many kids say the Magic Kingdom is the most special part of the World.

You can spend lots of time in its seven lands—Main Street, U.S.A., Adventureland, Frontierland, Liberty Square, Fantasyland, Mickey's Toontown Fair, and Tomorrowland. This chapter will help you decide which attractions you want to see first. Then flip back to page 14. It has tips on how to make a simple Magic Kingdom schedule. That way you can organize your visit and avoid wasting precious time.

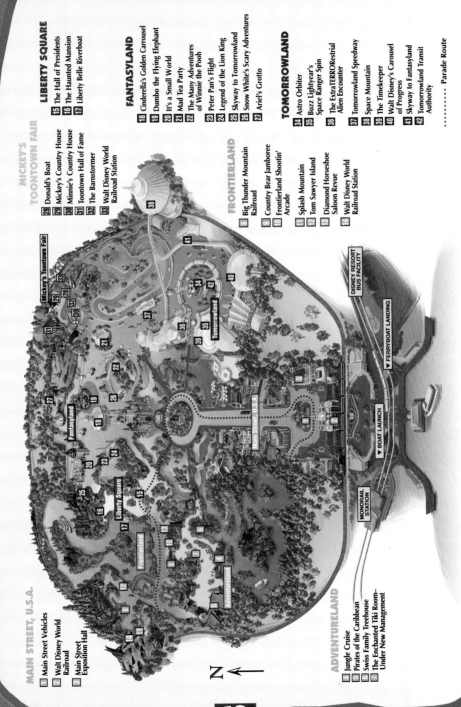

MAIN STREET, U.S.A.

1 Main Street Vehicles
2 Walt Disney World Railroad
3 Main Street Exposition Hall

ADVENTURELAND

4 Jungle Cruise
5 Pirates of the Caribbean
6 Swiss Family Treehouse
7 The Enchanted Tiki Room— Under New Management

MICKEY'S TOONTOWN FAIR

28 Donald's Boat
29 Mickey's Country House
30 Minnie's Country House
31 Toontown Hall of Fame
32 The Barnstormer
33 Walt Disney World Railroad Station

FRONTIERLAND

8 Big Thunder Mountain Railroad
9 Country Bear Jamboree
10 Frontierland Shootin' Arcade
11 Splash Mountain
12 Tom Sawyer Island
13 Diamond Horseshoe Saloon Revue
14 Walt Disney World Railroad Station

LIBERTY SQUARE

15 The Hall of Presidents
16 The Haunted Mansion
17 Liberty Belle Riverboat

FANTASYLAND

18 Cinderella's Golden Carrousel
19 Dumbo the Flying Elephant
20 It's a Small World
21 Mad Tea Party
22 The Many Adventures of Winnie the Pooh
23 Peter Pan's Flight
24 Legend of the Lion King
25 Skyway to Tomorrowland
26 Snow White's Scary Adventures
27 Ariel's Grotto

TOMORROWLAND

34 Astro Orbiter
35 Buzz Lightyear's Space Ranger Spin
36 The ExtraTERRORestrial Alien Encounter
37 Tomorrowland Speedway
38 Space Mountain
39 The Timekeeper
40 Walt Disney's Carousel of Progress
41 Skyway to Fantasyland
42 Tomorrowland Transit Authority

········· Parade Route

This is a map of the Magic Kingdom. You can get a bigger one at the park. They're free!

19

Main Street, U.S.A.

Are you ready for some time traveling? You'll do a lot of it in the Magic Kingdom. Four out of its seven lands send you either back or forward in time.

Main Street, U.S.A., is one of those lands. It was made to look like a small American town in the year 1900. (Some of it is based on the town Walt Disney grew up in—Marceline, Missouri.)

There are pretty lampposts, horse-drawn trolleys, and many other touches that make the street charming. If you look both ways before crossing, you'll notice a big difference between this Main Street and a real one: There's a castle at the end of it!

There are no major rides or attractions here, but Main Street, U.S.A, is still a fun place to be. You can sink your teeth into a fresh-baked cookie, hop aboard a train, or sit on the curb and watch a parade go by.

Walt Disney World Railroad

Walt Disney loved trains. He even had a miniature one in his backyard that was big enough to ride on.

The Magic Kingdom trains are real locomotives that were built nearly a hundred years ago. A full trip takes about 20 minutes, but you can get on or off at any station (at Main Street, U.S.A., Frontierland, or Mickey's Toontown Fair).

What do the kids who worked on this book think about the railroad? They love traveling by train. You get a great view of the park—plus a chance to rest your feet.

ONE WAY TRANSPORTATION

HOT

The names of important Disney workers are written on the windows of Main Street buildings. Look for Walt's name above the ice cream shop.

TIP

Main Street Vehicles

The railroad isn't the only transportation on Main Street, U.S.A. Horse-drawn trolleys, old-fashioned cars, and an antique fire engine make trips up and down the street throughout the day.

You can climb aboard any one of these vehicles in Town Square or by Cinderella Castle. Each trip is strictly one-way—you'll be asked to hop off after the ride.

The vehicles don't operate every day. Go to City Hall (on Main Street) to find out when they are running.

When the horses that pull the trolleys are taking a break, you'll usually find them in the Car Barn near City Hall. Stop in for a visit.

♥**HIDDEN MICKEY ALERT!** Look closely at the horse's bridle gear when you ride the Main Street Trolley.

Adventureland

A trip to Adventureland is like a visit to a tropical island. It has so many plants and trees that George of the Jungle would feel right at home. (Don't bother looking for him. He prefers his own treehouse to the one here. Besides, he probably couldn't find it if he tried.)

As you can tell from the name of this land, the attractions take you on exciting (and silly) adventures.

Jungle Cruise

It's a good thing elephants aren't shy. Otherwise, they might get upset when you watch them take a bath. That's just one of the interesting sights on the Jungle Cruise.

The voyage goes through the jungles of Africa and Asia. Along the way you see life-like zebras, giraffes, lions, hippos, and a few headhunters. (Don't worry—the only real animals in the ride are the humans inside the boat!)

If you love corny jokes, you'll definitely love this ride. The captain tells a bunch of them.

Some kids wish the ride were more exciting. "I love the ride," says Robert. "But it would be even cooler if the headhunters threw their spears."

The Jungle Cruise is usually very crowded—try to get there early in the morning. It's best to ride during the day, when you can see everything.

LINE GAMES

You might think these fellows would catch a cold playing chess in a dungeon so drafty and old. Can you find them?

Magic Kingdom

Pirates of the Caribbean

Ahoy, there, maties! There's rough waters ahead! That's the warning a pirate gives near the start of this attraction. He must be a wimpy pirate, because kids don't think this ride is rough at all. (But there is a small dip and some dark scenes, so be prepared.)

The journey takes place in a little boat. After floating through a quiet cave ... *BOOM!* You're in the middle of a pirate attack! Cannons blast while the song "Yo Ho, Yo Ho; a Pirate's Life for Me" plays over and over again. Watch for a pirate with his leg hanging over a bridge—the leg is really hairy.

Most kids give the pirates a thumbs-up. "This ride is fun for kids of all ages," says David G. Eric thinks "little kids might be scared. Especially if they aren't ready for the drop." Grace agrees. "The cannons and fire might be too scary, because everything looks so realistic, but that's what I like about it," she says.

23

HIDDEN MICKEY ALERT! Keep your eyes peeled for a Mickey head formed by three gold plates in the final scene of the Pirates.

Swiss Family Treehouse

What would it be like for your family to be stranded on an island? John Wyss asked his kids this question before he wrote a book called *The Swiss Family Robinson*. Together they came up with lots of crazy adventures for the Robinsons. They survive a shipwreck, fight off pirates, and build the most awesome treehouse in the world.

Just like the movie

Walt Disney Productions made a movie based on the book in 1960. The Swiss Family Treehouse in Adventureland looks just like the treehouse in the film. In it, you climb a staircase to many different levels. Each room has lots to see. The tree itself looks very real, but it's not. It has 300,000 plastic leaves, and concrete roots.

An excellent story

Everyone agrees that reading the story or seeing the movie *Swiss Family Robinson* makes the treehouse more fun to explore. "Once you know the story, the treehouse is fascinating," says David B. "I like the boys' room with the hammocks and the running water."

Robert knows the story, so he understood what he was seeing. "I could name all the rooms as we walked around," he says. "It's an excellent treehouse."

HOT  **TIP**

You'll get a kick out of this show if you like the movies Aladdin and The Lion King.

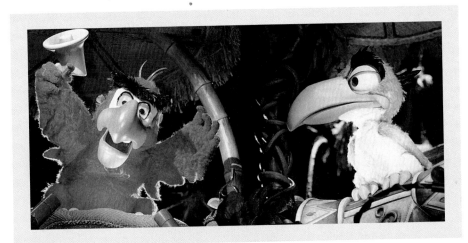

Magic Kingdom

The Enchanted Tiki Room— Under New Management

Birds rule at this attraction. They also sing and crack lots of jokes. If you've been here before, you may know José, Michael, Fritz, and Pierre. They've been singing old favorites, like "The Tiki, Tiki, Tiki Room," for more than 25 years.

Now the Tikis are "Under New Management." They have a new show and new bosses. One is Iago, who's as loud and cranky as he was in *Aladdin*. The other is the very nervous Zazu from *The Lion King*. Thanks to Iago, Zazu has plenty to worry about in the Tiki Room.

It seems Iago hasn't just joined the show—he has taken over! Zazu warns that changes might make the Tiki gods angry. But Iago just laughs.

Suddenly, the Tiki goddess of disaster appears. Her name is Uh Oa, and she is very angry. Zap! She shows Iago who's really boss—and makes him disappear.

Now it's the Tiki gods' turn to prove that they can sing as well as the birdies sing. Iago is allowed back to see the gods perform a hip-hop song—and he becomes their biggest fan.

25

♥**HIDDEN MICKEY ALERT!** Look for a Mickey or two on the bird perches inside the Tiki Room.

Frontierland

Howdy, pardners! And welcome to the Wild West. Frontierland shows you what America was like when pioneers first settled west of the Mississippi River. It's also where you'll find two of the best rides in the Magic Kingdom. Both of them are special Disney mountains. You can take a watery trip down Splash Mountain and ride a runaway train at Big Thunder Mountain Railroad. These are just a few of the fun things to do here.

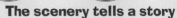

Splash Mountain

After riding Splash Mountain, you'll know how it got its name. It's impossible to stay dry! There are three small dips, leading up to a giant, watery drop.

You're all wet

Jennifer loves getting wet. That's why she likes to sit in the front seat when she rides Splash Mountain. "You *will* get wet, especially if you ride up front," she says. You don't get as soaked in the back, but "you feel airborne," Kirsti says.

The scenery tells a story

The kids agree that you have to go on it a few times before you can understand the ride's story. (You travel through scenes from Walt Disney's movie *Song of the South*.) Lindsay says, "Every time there's a little splash, something different happens to Brer Rabbit." Brad says, "Brer Rabbit is supposed to be in the log getting away from the fox and the bear." When the rabbit goes over the edge toward

Magic Kingdom

the end, you go along for the ride. (Try to keep your eyes open during the big drop—it won't be easy.)

Tate thinks that following the story "makes the ride even better." Karyn agrees. "All the characters are so cute and so detailed, and of course, the last drop is great."

You must be at least 40 inches tall to ride.

If you sit in the front or on the right side of the log, you get really wet!

Around here Brer Rabbit is a famous hare. You might guess why if you find this lair. Can you spot it?

LINE GAMES

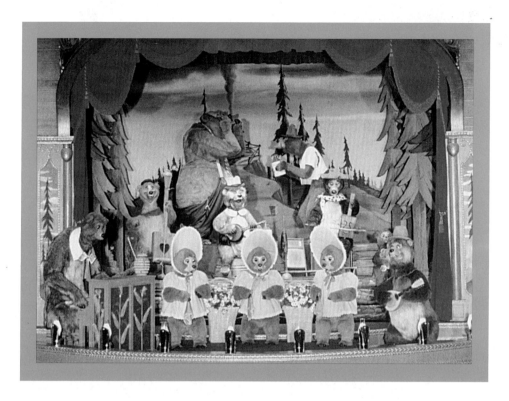

Country Bear Jamboree

You've never seen bears quite like these. They sing songs, play instruments, and tell jokes. This is a silly show, so be sure to go in with a silly attitude. Big Al is one of the most popular bears. And he can't even carry a tune!

Everyone gets in on the act

Sometimes the audience sings and claps along with the performers. Even the furry heads on the wall get into the act. (Melvin the moose, Buff the buffalo, and Buck the deer like to *hang* around the theater.)

What do kids think of the bears?

The country music show gets mixed reviews from kids. Some love it. Others aren't so thrilled. "It's a good show for little kids," says Eric.

Karyn agrees, saying she would rather spend her time on other rides. "But I think some kids would like to sing along with the characters," she adds.

Brian L. thinks "the bears are great, and some of them are funny. The one that can't sing is really funny. It's a very enjoyable show."

Tom Sawyer Island is quiet, but it's still rockin'—Teeter-Totter rock is a fun surprise to search for.

Tom Sawyer Island

There's only one way to get to Tom Sawyer Island—by raft. That's the way Tom himself used to travel. (He is a character created by the author Mark Twain.)

Don't expect to find any rides here. In fact, compared to the rest of the Magic Kingdom, it's pretty calm. But if you bring your imagination, you can have exciting adventures.

Bouncy bridges and secret exits

The island has a real windmill to wander through, hills to climb, and two neat bridges. One of them is an old barrel bridge. When one person bounces on it, everyone does.

Across one bridge is a wooden fort. It has air guns that you can shoot. And there's a secret exit that is really a path through a dark and narrow cave.

In all, there are three caves to explore. They are the best things on the island. Beware: The caves are very dark and a little scary.

Younger kids love it here

All of Tom Sawyer Island is popular with younger kids. Older kids think the bridges and caves are the best part.

If you get hungry, stop by Aunt Polly's Dockside Inn for a snack. The pickles are delicious!

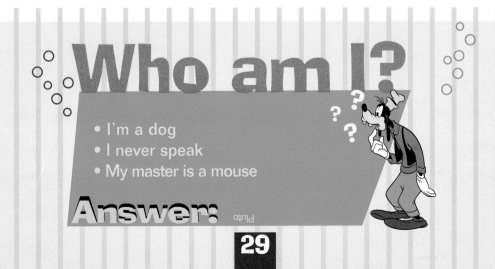

Who am I?

- I'm a dog
- I never speak
- My master is a mouse

Answer: Pluto

LINE GAMES

Throughout the mount folks once could hear the clanking of this "mining gear." Can you find it?

Big Thunder Mountain Railroad

ROUGH Attraction Reaction

Hang on to your hat, because this is one of the wildest rides in the wilderness. The speedy trains zip in, out, and over a huge mountain. They pass through scenes with real-looking chickens, goats, donkeys, and more.

A calmer coaster

The swoops and turns make this a thrilling roller coaster, but it's a lot tamer than Space Mountain. It's a ride you can go on again and again, and see new things each time. Look for funny sights in the town—like the poor guy floating around in a bathtub. Try to ride during the day and again at night.

Scream your head off

Kids have good things to say about this ride. "There are lots of fast turns and drops," says Jennifer. Justin says, "It's not too scary, but I was screaming because it's so much fun." David G. agrees. "I just love screaming and putting my hands in the air during the dips," he says.

You must be at least 40 inches tall to ride.

Who am I?

- I'm an excellent swimmer
- I never wear pants
- Huey, Dewey, and Louie call me Uncle

Answer: Donald Duck

More Frontierland Fun!

At the **Frontierland Shootin' Arcade**, you can aim at targets like tombstones and skulls. (You have to pay extra to use the arcade. It's not included in your Magic Kingdom park admission.)

A crew of singers and dancers performs all day at the **Diamond Horseshoe Saloon Revue**. The jokes are silly, but the show is a lot of fun. Sometimes people from the audience can even be in the show. If you want to get in on the act, sit near the front. If you have stage fright, it's best to watch from the balcony!

Liberty Square

LINE GAMES

Lying beneath the trees and stones is a brother named Claude who's nothing but bones. Can you find him?

What did America look like in colonial days? Parts of it looked like Liberty Square! This small area separates Frontierland from Fantasyland. It's a quiet spot with some shops and a couple of popular attractions.

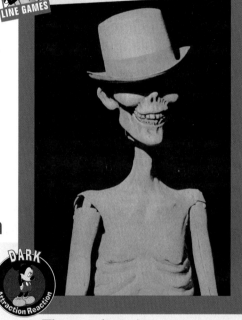

The Haunted Mansion

This haunted house isn't too scary, but there are plenty of ghosts to keep you on your toes. Before you enter, read the funny tombstones outside. (We love the one that says: Here lies brother Fred. A great big rock fell on his head.)

Once inside, you'll be stranded in a room with no windows and no doors. For a while, it seems like there's no way out.

DARK
Attraction Reaction

You are doomed

There's a moment before you board your "Doom Buggy" when the room is totally dark. It only lasts a few seconds, but for some, it's much too long.

The car doesn't move very fast, but it's still hard to catch all of the details. Watch for the door knockers that knock by themselves, a ghostly teapot pouring tea, and a ghost napping under the table at a party in the ballroom.

Fun for everyone

This ride is popular with people of all ages. Some parts are spooky, but in a fun way. "I was tense because it was my first time, but it wasn't that scary after all," says Eric.

Magic Kingdom

The Hall of Presidents

The first part of this attraction is a film about our government. Then the screen rises and all of the American presidents are on the stage together. They are Audio-Animatronics, but they look real. Can you find President Bill Clinton in the photo above?

Abraham Lincoln and Bill Clinton actually speak. (Mr. Clinton recorded the voice himself. Abraham Lincoln's voice is performed by an actor.) If you watch closely, you'll notice the presidents move, whisper, and even doze off.

The kids were pleasantly surprised by this attraction. Danielle G. says, "I thought it would be boring, but it isn't." Lindsay agrees. "It's a fun way to learn," she says.

Liberty Belle Riverboat

The Liberty Belle Riverboat docks in Liberty Square. This big steamboat takes guests on slow, relaxing cruises. It can be a nice break on a hot day. The best seats are right up front or in the back, where you can see both sides of the river as you go along.

Mickey's Toontown Fair

Looking for that world-famous mouse? You're sure to find him at Mickey's Toontown Fair. He has a job here and, of course, he does it well.

This is the newest land in the Magic Kingdom. It must be a great place because Mickey, Minnie, and their friends all have country homes here. Everywhere you look, you see colorful tents. That's because the county fair is always in town. Guess who's the head judge. (Hint: Think of the Mouse who does a good job.)

To get here, follow the path from the Mad Tea Party or from Space Mountain. Or take a ride on the Walt Disney World Railroad. It's a short trip and, if you ask Michael, it's worth it. "I think all kids will like it here," he says.

HOT

Mickey's Toontown Fair is a great place to meet the characters.

TIP

The Barnstormer

The only ride in Toontown Fair is the roller coaster at Goofy's Wiseacre Farm. The ride may look small, but it packs plenty of thrills. "I like the part where you go sideways really fast," Szasha says.

If you climb into a "plane," you'll zip through the farm. But watch out! You're about to crash into Goofy's barn. The hole in the wall tells you that someone has been there before you. Yes, it's clumsy old Goofy.

Before you ride The Barnstormer spend some time exploring Goofy's farm. Some of his vegetables are pretty wacky, just like him. Keep your eye out for the "bell" peppers and the "pop" corn. Then look up. Only Goofy would park his airplane in a water tower!

Magic Kingdom

Donald's Boat

A popular stop in Toontown is Donald's Boat. It's called the *Miss Daisy* and it's full of leaks. When you pull the whistle, water shoots out the top. To get to the boat, cross the "duck pond"— another great spot to get wet.

Mickey's Country House

The door is open, so come on in! Mickey's house tells you a lot about him. His game room is full of sports stuff. But the kitchen is a mess. That's what happens when you let Donald and Goofy decorate!

Where's Mickey? He's hard at work in the Judge's Tent. Walk out the back door of the house and follow the path. You can't miss it! On your way, check out Mickey's garden. Even the vegetables have mouse ears.

Judge's Tent

You found him! Mickey is here all day long, ready to have his picture taken with you. There's always a long wait, but the line is shorter late in the day.

Minnie's Country House

Go ahead, climb on the furniture—Minnie won't mind. There's lots to see and touch in this house. Press the button on Minnie's answering machine and listen to her messages. Open the refrigerator, and feel the cold air. And get set for a trick when you try to take a chocolate chip cookie off her table.

Grace thinks younger kids will love Minnie's house "because there's so much to do. You can play with everything in her kitchen. I like the microwave oven!" she says.

Once you've explored inside, head for Minnie's backyard. She is a very good gardener. On your way there, look at the funny flowers in the sun room. The palm tree has hands, the tiger lilies have tiger faces, and the tulips all have two lips!

Toontown Hall of Fame

This tent is filled with winning entries from the fair and goodies to buy. But the best reason to come here is to meet the characters. They are hanging out in three different rooms. You have to stand in a separate line to enter each room. The sign shows which characters are in each room, so you'll know which line to get in.

Mystery Mouse

What did Walt Disney almost name Mickey Mouse? To find out, complete this Walt Disney World word puzzle. First fill in the blanks below. Then write your answers in the grid. (All of the answers appear somewhere in this book.) The mystery name will magically appear in the shaded area. Good luck!

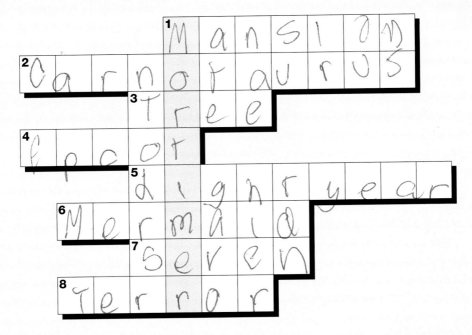

1. 999 happy haunts live in the Haunted_____.
2. The_____is a scary dinosaur in Countdown to Extinction.
3. The_____of Life is 145 feet tall.
4. Future World and World Showcase are in_____.
5. Buzz_____stars in a new Magic Kingdom attraction.
6. The Little_____sings in a show at the Disney-MGM Studios.
7. There are_____lands in the Magic Kingdom.
8. Guests fall 13 stories on the Twilight Zone Tower of_____.

Fantasyland

Fantasyland is home to a lot of magical rides that younger kids just love. Older kids and even grown-ups enjoy them, too. These attractions are very popular, and the waits can be long. But the lines are usually shorter while people are watching the afternoon parade. So it's a good idea to skip the parade one day and visit Fantasyland. Plan to catch the parade on another day.

Ariel's Grotto

There is a mysterious blue cave tucked behind Dumbo the Flying Elephant. Inside, there is a special surprise—and her name is Ariel. The star of *The Little Mermaid* is waiting to meet you in her grotto (grotto is another word for cave). Ask her to autograph this book on page 160.

Out front, there are some fountains to play in, so it's a great place to get wet.

Szasha says, "If you really like Ariel, you should definitely go." She also likes the "funny rocks that squirt water." Danielle T. has this advice: "Try to go when it's not so crowded, or you may have to wait a long time."

Cinderella's Golden Carrousel

Just about all of the attractions at Walt Disney World were dreamed up by Disney Imagineers. But not the carousel. It was discovered in New Jersey, where it was once part of another amusement park. It was built around 1917.

When you climb on a horse for your ride on the carousel, be sure to notice that each one is different. And remember to look up at the ceiling and its hand-painted scenes from *Cinderella*. While you ride, enjoy famous Disney tunes, including "Zip-A-Dee-Doo-Dah," "When You Wish Upon a Star," and "Be Our Guest."

"You can never grow too old for a carousel," says Lissy. "The horses are beautiful and the music makes it great." Robert agrees. "I love the carousel and I love the music. I think people of any age would like it."

Mad Tea Party

The idea for the giant teacups that spin through this ride came from a scene in *Alice in Wonderland*. In the movie, the Mad Hatter throws himself a tea party to celebrate his un-birthday. That's any day that *isn't* his birthday!

You control the spin

On the Mad Tea Party ride, you control how fast your cup spins by turning the big wheel in the center. The more you turn, the more you spin. Or you can just sit back and let the cup spin on its own. It may be hard while you're whirling, but try to take a peek at the little mouse who keeps popping out of the big teapot in the center.

"It's a very good ride and it really makes you dizzy," says Nita. Brian L. agrees. "I wish it would go even faster, but it's good that you spin as fast or as slow as you want," he says.

It takes teamwork

For the best ride, David B. suggests that everyone in the cup try to work together. "You have to coordinate," he says. "Sometimes you can go faster if fewer people work at spinning the wheel."

Most kids agree that the ride is too short (it lasts about two minutes). Lissy doesn't mind, though. "Your arms get tired after a while," says Lissy, "but the teacups are always fun."

LINE GAMES

Can you spot three storks in a row? They don't need big ears to fly like Dumbo.

READER TIP

"There is always a mad rush for Dumbo, so get there very early!"

Jessica (age 12)
Staten Island, NY

Magic Kingdom

Dumbo the Flying Elephant

Just like the star of the movie *Dumbo*, these elephants know how to fly. They'd love to take you for a short ride (about two minutes) above Fantasyland. A button lets you control the up and down movement of the elephant.

Take your kid brother

Many of the kids agree that this ride is more fun for younger kids from ages 3 to 8. But they all find something to like, and think it would be fun to go on with a younger brother or sister.

Brian L. also suggests it for younger kids. "It's not a bad ride, and I think little kids would love it," he says. Robert likes "to go up really high. I think some kids might be scared of the height, though."

Beware of long lines

Even though Disney added more Dumbos a few years ago, lines for this attraction tend to be long. Anna thinks the ride is "way too short. But if you don't wait in line too long, it's fun to go on."

Danielle G. loves it. "It has the appearance of a child's ride, but it's fun for everyone," she says. Tate agrees. "Most people think it's just for little kids, but it's fun."

DARK
Attraction Reaction

Peter Pan's Flight

Swoop and soar through scenes that tell the story of how Wendy, Michael, and John get sprinkled with pixie dust and fly off to Never Land with Peter Pan and Tinker Bell. Along the way you meet up with Princess Tiger Lily, the evil Captain Hook, and his sidekick Mr. Smee.

Near the beginning of the trip, there's a beautiful scene of London at night. Notice that the cars on the streets really move. Later, watch out for the crocodile who wants to eat Captain Hook.

When you first board your pirate ship, it seems like you're riding on a track on the ground. Once you get going the track is actually above you, so it feels like the ship is really flying.

"I love this ride and how it makes you feel like you can fly," says Robert. "I especially like the part at the end with the crocodile."

Jennifer thinks "It's fun to look down at London below and see all the small cars and bright city lights."

David B. points out that Peter Pan's Flight is different from all the other Fantasyland rides because "you're hooked from the top instead of being on a track below you." He adds, "I never get tired of this ride."

Magic Kingdom

It's a Small World

People have a lot in common, no matter where they live. That's the point of this attraction. In it, you take a slow boat ride through several large rooms where beautiful dolls represent different parts of the world. There are Greek dancers, Japanese kite flyers, Scottish bagpipers, and many more. There's also a jungle scene with hippos, giraffes, and monkeys.

All this colorful scenery is set to the song "It's a Small World." Pay attention to the costumes on the dolls, and try to guess which

country they're from. Nita says, "The costumes are adorable, and I like the faces on the dolls. But the ride is too slow. If it had a few dips, it would be better."

David G. does think the ride is "slow moving, but it's fun at the same time." Jennifer agrees. "It's a nice, relaxing boat ride after a long day in the theme parks," she says.

It's a Small World is loved by people of all ages. That's why it's one of the most famous rides in Walt Disney World. As Eric says, "I would hope that everyone likes it, even if the song is a little bit repetitive!"

The Many Adventures of Winnie the Pooh

Winnie the Pooh loves his honey. In fact, he'll do anything to keep the sweet treat safe. On this dizzying trip through the Hundred Acre Wood, see what Pooh must do to rescue his honey pots and his friends, too.

The Blustery Day

The wind is howling, the leaves are rustling and everything in Pooh's world is blowing away. Roo and Piglet are up in the air. Even Owl's house is about to topple over. You better hang on to your honey pot, or you may be swept off next!

A Sticky Situation

Finally the wind calms and Pooh can get to sleep. But when he wakes up from his silly dream, it's raining out. Pooh's honey pots are about to wash away. He can save them, but will he save himself?

Everyone loves Pooh

This attraction replaced Mr. Toad's Wild Ride. Some kids were sad to say good-bye to Mr. Toad. But everyone agrees that Winnie the Pooh is a good addition. Unlike Mr. Toad, this ride is fun for kids of all different ages. Even grown-ups love Pooh, so the lines may be long.

Snow White's Scary Adventures

This attraction takes you through scenes from the movie *Snow White and the Seven Dwarfs*. Some scenes are sweet, while others are scary. If you like Snow White, you're in luck. She is in a lot of scenes (but so is the nasty old witch). Don't expect to see much of the dwarfs—they don't show up a lot.

There are lots of turns, and the witch seems to be around each one of them. It's very dark during most of the ride, so it can get pretty creepy—especially for younger kids.

The kids aren't sure who this ride is meant for. It's too scary for many small children and a little simple for older kids.

David G. says, "This ride focuses too much on the wicked witch." Grace agrees. "There are not enough scenes of Snow White and the dwarfs. Make sure you look at the warning sign before you get on the ride. It might be very scary for some kids," she adds.

Magic Kingdom

Can you find some squirrels by chance? They're running, but not from branch to branch.

LINE GAMES

45

HIDDEN MICKEY ALERT! Notice the rocks in the Lion King theater. They form a Mickey head.

Legend of the Lion King

Disney's hit movie comes to life in Legend of the Lion King. This show uses animation, life-size puppets, special effects, and music to tell the story of Simba and his friends from the movie.

When the sun rises over Pride Rock, Mufasa and Simba make their big entrance. The characters may look life-like, but they are really large puppets.

Sing "Hakuna Matata"

As the story continues, other characters act out parts of the movie. Special effects, like water mists and wind, make the theater seem like a jungle. During the stampede scene, the room rumbles. Of course, no Lion King show would be complete without a visit from Timon and Pumbaa. When they sing "Hakuna Matata," feel free to sing along!

Kids agree

All the kids agree that this is a great show. Dan says he loves all the special effects, "like the steam shooting up on the stage and the light rain." David G. enjoys the show because it "combines live action and clips from the movie on stage." Michael just loves everything about it. "It's the best play I've ever seen," he says.

The line for the Skyway is usually shorter in Tomorrowland.

Skyway to Tomorrowland

Drifting along in a Skyway car is the next best thing to flying. The ride lifts guests high in the air above the Magic Kingdom. It runs between Fantasyland and Tomorrowland. All trips are one-way.

"It's fun," says Lindsay. "You get a really good view of the park and you can take pictures."

Dawna and Danielle G. both think the ride feels like a ski lift. Dawna offers this tip: "It's not a good ride if you're afraid of heights."

The Skyway is a popular ride with a slow-moving line. If you're in a rush, there's a much faster way to get places—your feet!

47

Tomorrowland

Tomorrowland began as a peek at the future. But as the real world changed, so did this land. Now, it's like a city from a science fiction story. The palm trees are made of metal. The rides here let you rocket through space or travel through time. And a scary alien even beams down for a visit! A good way to see this land is to ride on the Tomorrowland Transit Authority—it's cool and breezy and it never has a long line.

DARK Attraction Reaction **ROUGH** Attraction Reaction **SCARY** Attraction Reaction

Space Mountain

Thrill seekers like to head straight for this rocket ride through outer space. It has twists, turns, and steep dips. And it all takes place in the dark! It's one of the most popular rides in Walt Disney World.

Older kids love it

Danielle T. says, "I really felt like I was in a rocket going to space. This is one of the best rides." Jennifer agrees. "I like how it's all in the dark. The suspense makes it so much fun."

LINE GAMES

In darkness search to see this light.
It's from a comet burning bright.
Can you find it?

Nita has a warning: "It goes too fast. I'm not a roller coaster person, and I felt like I was about to fall out."

Is it too scary?

Everyone agrees: Space Mountain is scary! But some kids say it's a "good scary." Anything that was "bad scary" happened only in their imaginations.

Anna says, "The ride rattles a lot. I wish that there were higher sides to the cars." But don't worry: The coaster is perfectly safe. And, as David G. says, "Space Mountain is a must for all roller coaster fans!" Is it for you?

You must be at least 44 inches tall to ride.

Magic Kingdom

HOT

Never eat right
before going on
Space Mountain.

TIP!

♥**HIDDEN MICKEY ALERT!** While on line for this attraction, look for a Mickey hiding in the alien writing on the wall.

DARK
Attraction Reaction

LOUD
Attraction Reaction

SCARY
Attraction Reaction

The ExtraTERRORestrial Alien Encounter

People from another planet want to show off their new machine. They say it can beam people through space. But that's not what happens. Instead, an alien arrives and escapes into the audience. It's ugly and it's hungry. And it just might eat *you*!

It's not for everyone

That's the story of Alien Encounter, the Magic Kingdom's scariest attraction. Kids like this show a lot but say that it's not for everyone—especially younger kids. "The first time I went on it I was 10 and I cried," says Amy. "But I've always been a scaredy cat."

Brian F. says, "I did not go on it, because I don't like aliens. I went to the arcade instead." Lindsay feels just the opposite. She likes scary things and loves this attraction.

The alien licks your head

Jennifer says, "Don't be surprised if the alien licks you, breathes on you, or even touches you!"

Grace loves the effects. "Sit back in your seat to make sure you can feel the alien when he's behind you," she says. David G. also has a tip: "If you get too scared, just close your eyes!"

You must be at least 44 inches tall to enter Alien Encounter.

The Timekeeper

Travel through time with Timekeeper, one of the world's wackiest robots. In this attraction, he takes you on a tour of the past and the future.

Okay, you don't *really* time travel in this attraction—but it feels like you do. A robot named 9-Eye is the real time traveler. She takes pictures that fill the nine screens in the theater. A movie completely surrounds the audience.

It will make your head spin

When you watch the screens, it feels like you're moving. "This made me dizzy," says Lindsay. "But it still is sort of neat." Eric agrees. "The Timekeeper is really good. I especially liked the end. But don't go if your feet are tired—there are no seats, only rails to lean on."

Don't miss it

Grace says, "It's so funny that you don't even notice it's educational." Seth has a tip for kids who have never seen it before: "Don't forget to look behind you." Otherwise you might miss something.

Arcade Alert!

The **Tomorrowland Light & Power Co.** is a high-tech video arcade. It's right next to Space Mountain.

It's a good place to wait if you don't want to ride Space Mountain or go to Alien Encounter. Just like other arcades, you have to pay to play here.

Walt Disney's Carousel of Progress

A lot has changed since 1900. There was no electricity, water came from a well, and nobody had a TV. Life was rough! This attraction shows you how life has changed since then.

A look at American families

The show is called Carousel of Progress because you move in a circle, just like on a carousel. You pass different scenes along the way. Each one teaches a little history.

"I really appreciate the story," says Tate. "It's a down-to-earth look at how the American family has progressed over the years."

Learning can be fun

Anna finds it "a good way to learn. I think it's cool when they say, in the early scenes, how 'that will never happen,' and we know that it already has."

Adam W. likes "how we learn about all the inventions that were created in the years past."

Eric's favorite scene comes at the end. "It's so funny to see Granny playing the virtual reality game. It's neat to watch one family change over time."

What's your favorite scene in the Carousel of Progress?

♥**HIDDEN MICKEY ALERT!** The line for this ride takes you past a giant map of the planets. Look closely at each planet—Mickey's profile is in one of them.

HOT

To get more points, hold the button down the whole time, and aim at small, moving, or far away targets.

TIP

Buzz Lightyear's Space Ranger Spin

In this attraction, everyone is a toy—including you. In fact, you are so small, you fit inside a video game shooting gallery.

To infinity and beyond!

The ride is under the command of Buzz Lightyear. You've just become a Junior Space Ranger, so you're under his command, too. Together, you zoom through the galaxy and battle the evil Emperor Zurg.

Zap that Zurg

Zurg and his robots are stealing batteries from other toys. They plan to use the batteries to power their ultimate weapon of destruction. Your job is to fight back. Use the laser cannons in your spaceship to aim at the targets (they look like Z's) and zap Zurg's power. Every time you hit a target you earn more points. There is a scoreboard by your cannon that shows you how many points you've gotten. At the end of the ride, you'll pass a giant chart. It shows everyone's ranger rank based on their score. Check to see where your score falls. Most kids improve every time they ride.

Tomorrowland Speedway

You don't need a license to drive your own car around this racetrack (as long as you're 52 inches tall). Cars travel along a track, but it's not as easy to drive as it looks. Even experts bounce around a lot. The cars are real and are powered by gasoline.

Some of the kids really enjoy driving their own cars. "The race cars are fun because you get to steer them yourself," says Szasha. "I like the curves." Robert says, "I love it. I think it goes pretty fast and I like having my own car."

Karyn thinks the race cars could be a little more exciting. David B. agrees. "I like the ride," he says. "But I wish they didn't have the track in the middle."

Astro Orbiter

In the middle of Tomorrowland, there is a giant, glowing tower. It is called Rockettower. The Astro Orbiter ride is all the way at the top. In it, you soar past colorful planets high above Tomorrowland.

You can take the ride by yourself or with a friend. (Each rocket fits two people.) "This is a fun ride," says Eric, "and the view is very pretty at night." Dawna thinks, "People who don't have the stomach for Space Mountain can go. It still has the space theme."

Kirsti has a tip: "Sit in the front so you can control how high up you go."

READER TIP

"If you're afraid of heights, skip Astro Orbiter!"
Derek (age 13)
Spokane, WA

Take a Tour of Tomorrowland!

The **Tomorrowland Transit Authority** travels by or through most of the land's attractions. If you're not sure about going on Space Mountain, the view from here can help you decide. It's also interesting that the ride doesn't give off any pollution. Szasha says, "It takes you past the different rides so you can see what they are like before riding them." Eric says, "It gives you a nice, relaxing tour of Tomorrowland." Michael adds, "The announcer tells you about each ride. And it's a good place to rest."

If you would like to ride the **Skyway** cable cars that travel between Tomorrowland and Fantasyland, this is the best place to board. The lines at the Tomorrowland station are much shorter, so get on here.

Entertainment

The Magic Kingdom is a very entertaining place. It seems like there is always a show starting or a parade going by. Read on to learn about some of the special events that take place in the park. For more information, check a park guidemap. You can get one in any Disney resort, at the entrance to the park, or in the shops and restaurants.

MAIN STREET ELECTRICAL PARADE

You can only see this parade at night. That's because the floats glow in the dark! They are covered in more than 575,000 twinkling lights. Squint your eyes as the floats go by and the effect will be even better.

DISNEY'S MAGICAL MOMENTS PARADE

Your favorite Disney characters are on the march in this parade. Mickey and his pals want everyone to join in the fun. Danielle T. says, "I danced in the Cinderella scene. It was an experience I'll never forget!"

Each parade float has a surprise, like confetti or fireworks. Szasha has a tip: "Get a spot on the curb early. They may ask you to be in the parade."

FANTASY IN THE SKY FIREWORKS

Look—up in the sky! It's not a bird or a plane . . . it's the most amazing fireworks show you've ever seen! Hundreds of colorful bursts explode within seven minutes. For the best view of the show, stand right in the middle of Main Street, facing the castle.

Where to Find Characters at the Magic Kingdom

   Disney characters greet guests all over the Magic Kingdom. The best place to find them is **Mickey's Toontown Fair**. You can meet Mickey in the **Judge's Tent**, and the rest of the gang in the **Toontown Hall of Fame**.

   Characters from *The Jungle Book*, *Aladdin*, and *The Lion King* hang out at the entrance to **Adventureland**. Alice and her friends prefer **Fantasyland**, while Brer Fox and Brer Bear enjoy spending time at **Splash Mountain**.

   If you want to meet The Little Mermaid, go to **Ariel's Grotto** in Fantasyland. There are lots of fountains you can play in, too.

   To find out exactly where and when to meet your favorite characters, pick up a free park guidemap or ask a cast member.

MAGIC KINGDOM TIPS

Head to this park first, since it has the most rides for kids.

Arrive a half hour before the opening time. Walk down Main Street to get a head start for when the rest of the park opens.

Check the Tip Boards on Main Street, in Frontierland, and in Tomorrowland. They list the wait times for popular attractions.

Rest your feet and watch Mickey's first movie in the Exposition Hall on Main Street. Afterwards you can e-mail a photo of yourself to a friend or pose for pictures in front of funny backgrounds.

Need to cool off on a hot day? Stop by Ariel's Grotto in Fantasyland, Donald's Boat in Mickey's Toontown Fair, or Cool Ship in Tomorrowland. You can get soaked with water at all of these places.

If the park is open late, it's fun to go on your favorite attractions again after dark.

There are "chicken exits" in the lines for all scary rides, just in case you change your mind about riding at the last minute.

Never eat just before riding The Barnstormer, Astro Orbiter, Space Mountain, Big Thunder Mountain Railroad, or the Mad Tea Party.

If you've never been on a roller coaster, ride The Barnstormer first. If you like it, try Big Thunder Mountain Railroad next. Save Space Mountain for last—it's the scariest.

If there are two lines at an attraction, the one on the left is usually shorter.

Attraction Ratings

COOL
(Check It Out)

- Cinderella's Golden Carrousel
- Snow White's Scary Adventures
- The Hall of Presidents
- The Timekeeper
- Tomorrowland Transit Authority
- Walt Disney World Railroad
- Liberty Belle Riverboat
- Swiss Family Treehouse

REALLY COOL
(Don't Miss)

- The Barnstormer
- Astro Orbiter
- Tomorrowland Speedway
- The Enchanted Tiki Room—Under New Management
- Mad Tea Party
- Country Bear Jamboree
- Jungle Cruise
- It's a Small World
- Carousel of Progress
- Tom Sawyer Island
- Dumbo the Flying Elephant
- Skyway

THE COOLEST
(See at Least Twice)

- Space Mountain
- Splash Mountain
- Big Thunder Mountain Railroad
- The Haunted Mansion
- Peter Pan's Flight
- Alien Encounter
- Buzz Lightyear's Space Ranger Spin
- Pirates of the Caribbean
- Legend of the Lion King
- The Many Adventures of Winnie the Pooh

Magic Kingdom

What do YOU think?

The kids who worked on this book rated all the attractions at Walt Disney World. But your opinion counts, too! Make your own "Attraction Ratings" list for each park and send it to us. We'll use it when we create next year's book. (Our address is on page 6.)

Epcot

Epcot is a great place to make discoveries about the world. And this year there's even more to learn, because Epcot is home to Disney's special Millennium Celebration. Every day will be a party!

The attractions at Epcot are in buildings called pavilions. The pavilions are in two sections of the park. One section is **Future World**, and the other is **World Showcase**. Future World celebrates cool inventions and ideas. It shows how they affect everything, from the land and sea to your mind and body.

World Showcase lets you travel around the world without leaving the park! There are many different countries to visit here. Each country has copies of its famous buildings, restaurants, and other landmarks. Together, they make you feel as if you're visiting the real place.

WORLD SHOWCASE

- MOROCCO
- FRANCE
- JAPAN
- THE AMERICAN ADVENTURE
- INTERNATIONAL GATEWAY
- UNITED KINGDOM
- ITALY
- MILLENNIUM VILLAGE
- GERMANY
- AMERICA GARDENS THEATRE
- WORLD SHOWCASE LAGOON
- CANADA
- IMAGINATION!
- CHINA
- NORWAY
- THE LAND
- **FUTURE WORLD**
- SHOWCASE PLAZA
- MEXICO
- INNOVENTIONS WEST
- THE LIVING SEAS
- TEST TRACK
- INNOVENTIONS EAST
- MILLENNIUM CENTRAL
- SPACESHIP EARTH
- To Buses
- WONDERS OF LIFE
- UNIVERSE OF ENERGY
- LEAVE A LEGACY
- Entrance Plaza

N

61

Epcot is a big place. Use this map to help plan your trip through the park.

Future World

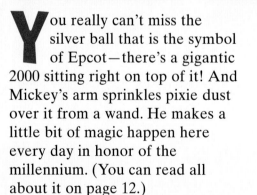

When you enter Epcot by monorail, you are in the area called Future World. Many of the attractions here are educational—but that doesn't mean you won't have fun. Take it from other kids: There's a lot to explore.

SPACESHIP EARTH

DARK Attraction Reaction

You really can't miss the silver ball that is the symbol of Epcot—there's a gigantic 2000 sitting right on top of it! And Mickey's arm sprinkles pixie dust over it from a wand. He makes a little bit of magic happen here every day in honor of the millennium. (You can read all about it on page 12.)

The Spaceship Earth ride is inside this big, round building. The ride shows you the different ways people have communicated over the years.

A highlight of the trip is when your time machine vehicle reaches the top of the building. Look up and you'll think you are staring into a night sky. The stars are beautiful.

Older kids enjoy this attraction. Ashley P. didn't like the ride when she was younger, but "now it's much more interesting to me," she says.

After the ride, check out the Global Neighborhood. There are games and other fun activities. They teach you about new ways to communicate with each other.

♥**HIDDEN MICKEY ALERT!** This time he's i
the stars. Look for him as you board the

Chill out!

INNOVENTIONS

Here's your chance to test out some exciting new inventions. You may also surf the Internet, send a video postcard to a friend by e-mail, or learn how to make pancakes from wood pulp.

On the road again

At Innoventions you travel down "The Road to Tomorrow." Along the way, stop at each of the interesting exhibits. Some of them teach you about new technologies, while others show you recent inventions for the home or tell you about discoveries in science. New inventions are brought in every three months or so. As Ashley J. says, "The place changes all the time, so you can come again and again." But no matter when you come, you'll get a taste of the future.

Need a place to escape from the heat? Head to Ice Station Cool in Innoventions Plaza. The entrance is an arctic chamber that's so cold it has real snow in it all year long! Inside you can sample sodas from all different countries for free. Some are delicious, but most kids think one tastes terrible. Are you brave enough to sample them all?

Street smarts

Tom Morrow 2.0 is your tour guide at Innoventions. He's an Audio-Animatronics robot who will keep you from getting lost during your trip. There are road signs and street maps, too. Still can't find what you are looking for? Simply ask a cast member to lead you on your way.

You'll get a better view of the manatees during the day. The light in their tank is dimmed at night so they can sleep.

THE LIVING SEAS

There's something fishy about the animals at The Living Seas. They aren't like any of the other animals in Future World. These critters are all real!

There are more than 2,000 sea creatures living here. It's the world's largest aquarium. There are turtles, dolphins, manatees, and even sharks.

Under the sea

Your sea exploration begins with a short movie. It explains how the earth's oceans were formed. Next, you get in a "hydrolator" (an elevator that goes in water) to go down to see the aquarium. As you get out, ask your parents how deep they think the hydrolator went. Then tell them it moved less than one inch!

Hands-on fun

After a quick ride through the aquarium, you enter an area called Sea Base Alpha. This is your chance to take a closer look at the creatures and to try out the hands-on exhibits.

"The Living Seas is really cool," says Robert. "I thought my ears popped in the hydrolator. It feels like you're going way down to the bottom of the sea."

Brian L. likes the interactive exhibits. "You can put your arms in a diving suit and try to move like you're in the ocean," he says.

Karyn just loves the manatees. "The rest of the exhibits are okay," she says, "but I like to see animals."

♥HIDDEN MICKEY ALERT! Study the paintings while you wait in line for Living with the Land. One has bubbles on it that connect to form a Mickey head.

THE LAND

The building called The Land looks like a big greenhouse. The attractions inside focus on food and where it comes from. There's a boat ride, a funny show about food, and special guided tours. There's also a movie about the environment. It stars Simba, Timon, and Pumbaa from *The Lion King*.

Living with the Land

What's the most popular fruit on our planet? The banana! People eat more bananas than any other fruity snack. You'll learn lots more food facts on this boat trip. The boat travels through rooms that look like a rain forest, desert, and prairie. Then it heads to a greenhouse area.

A tour guide explains everything your boat floats past. If you're lucky, you'll see some giant vegetables growing here. The greenhouse has produced some of the biggest lemons and eggplants in the world!

In all, The Land grows more than 30 tons of fruit and veggies each year. A lot of it is served to guests in Epcot restaurants.

This boat ride scores high marks with kids. Lindsay says, "The greenhouses are amazing." Anna likes that "it shows us new ways to make the best of our earth."

Behind The Seeds Tour

Kids (and parents) who are interested in the environment can sign up for this one-hour guided tour of the growing areas at The Land. It costs $6 for adults, and $4 for kids ages 3 through 9. You'll need reservations. Make them at the front of the Green Thumb Emporium shop.

Food Rocks

Here's a different kind of rock concert with a lesson about good nutrition. These are performers you won't see on any other stage. They are popular musicians who have been turned into foods. They perform old songs with funny new words.

Follow your nose

In the pre-show area, look at the fun food facts painted on the walls. Open one of the "smell boxes" and get a strong whiff of chocolate, garlic, coffee, bacon, orange, or seafood. Dawna points out the carpeting, with its pattern of forks, knives, and spoons.

Eat right—or else!

Kids enjoy this show, but it's best for a younger audience. David G. says, "This is a fun way for little kids to learn about nutrition." Jennifer adds, "The music makes the subject more entertaining." Dawna thinks the show "makes you feel guilty for eating food that's not good for you."

Most of the kids like the names of the performers and the songs they sing. But some of the songs are old, and sometimes it's hard to make out the lyrics. "It's probably more appealing to adults who know the music," Grace says. "But I think it's a great idea."

Epcot

The Circle of Life

Simba, Timon, and Pumbaa are together again. This time they're in a movie about protecting the earth's environment. The film is a mix of animation and live action. It shows some of the problems we face — and how we can fix them.

Timber!

The movie's opening scene shows animals just like those in *The Lion King* (but these animals are real). Next you see Simba near a watering hole. All of a sudden he hears "Timber!" and is drenched by the splash of a tree falling into water. Timon and Pumbaa are clearing the grassland to build a resort (The Hakuna Matata Lakeside Village).

Simba tells a story

Simba remembers what his father taught him about caring for the land. He tells his friends a story about how humans sometimes forget that everything is connected in the great Circle of Life.

Brian F. gets the message of this film. "It means to recycle, don't pollute, and don't litter," he explains. "I like the pictures they took of the fish, birds, alligators, penguins, and bears. And the cartoons are funny."

For Emma, "this movie is a nice reminder about what happens when we forget about the Circle of Life." Ashley J. says, "It really makes you want to change everything. I'm going to recycle more!"

IMAGINATION!

This pavilion is like a workout for your mind—all of the attractions put your imagination to work! There is an interesting and fun ride that tests your imagination, and a wacky 3-D movie called Honey, I Shrunk the Audience. Outside, the jumping waters of the Leap Frog Fountains are sure to keep you guessing. There are a lot of other ways to have fun here, too. Just use your imagination!

Journey Into Your Imagination

Think how different the world would be without imagination in it. There would be no stories to tell, no pictures to draw, and no inventions to make things easier. One thing is for sure— Walt Disney World certainly wouldn't exist! Imagination is so important to Disney that they created a special place in Future World to learn all about it. It's called the Imagination Institute. Here you can go on a trip as far as your mind will take you.

Testing, testing 1-2-3

The Imagination Institute is having an open house. That means everyone is invited to see and learn about all of its secret projects. As a special guest, you may even be able to test out their latest invention—The Imaginator.

It's all in your head

The Imaginator promises to make you think and look at things in a whole new way. There are lots of special effects during the ride that make the tests even more interesting. Will The Imaginator be a success? That's up to you. If you want the experiments to work, just concentrate, and put *your* imagination to the test.

Are you a Figment fan? He's not the star of a ride anymore, but you can still spot him here. So be on the lookout!

Who am I?

- Pooh is my pal
- My tail is tacked on
- I like pink bows

Answer: Eeyore

Leap Frog Fountains

It's easy to guess where these fountains get their name. Streams of water leap from one garden to the next. Catch them if you can!

This area is a hit with kids of all ages. "If you stand in the right place, you can get totally wet," says Taran. "It's one of my favorite things."

Nita thinks it's neat "how the water jumps right over your head." Brian F. has "never seen fountains that do that before. They really do look like they're leaping over each other."

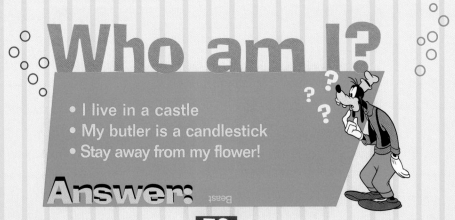

Who am I?

- I live in a castle
- My butler is a candlestick
- Stay away from my flower!

Answer: Beast

LINE GAMES

In darkness when you want to see, use these and electricity. Can you find them?

SCARY — Attraction Reaction

DARK — Attraction Reaction

LOUD — Attraction Reaction

Honey, I Shrunk the Audience

Remember the kids from *Honey, I Shrunk the Kids*? This 3-D movie gives you an idea of how they felt. That's because this time, you're the one who gets shrunk, along with the rest of the audience. Even the theater seems to shrink.

You get spooked by 3-D mice, a lion, and a scary snake. Then one of the kids from the movie picks up the theater and carries it around. Somehow you're brought back to real size, but only after some unusual adventures.

Very special effects

As Brian F. tells it, "First the professor shrinks himself. Then he accidentally hits the laser and shrinks us! The people on the screen are really big." Emma adds, "It makes you feel really small."

Brian F. says, "When the 3-D mice come out, it seems like they are really there. It's cool." Ashley J. also finds the effects believable. "I even put my feet up!" she says.

Some scary moments

"This is a very neat experience," says Lindsay. "But some parts might be scary for little kids."

Tate says, "This attraction really gives you the feeling that you're shrinking. There's a neat twist at the end." But we won't tell you what it is. As Emma puts it, "I don't want to give any more away. It's nice having a surprise."

HOT

If your hair is long, put it in a ponytail before riding, or it might get all tangled up.

TIP

LINE GAMES

A dummy you would have to be to take this test of belt safety. Can you find it?

Epcot

TEST TRACK

What is it like to be a crash test dummy? Find out in this thrilling ride—and learn what new cars go through to be safe for riders.

Where are the brakes?

Test Track is Epcot's fastest ride. The sporty test cars travel on a track that's almost a mile long. Your car has no steering wheel or brake pedals, but its sound and video equipment lets you know what's being tested. You zip around curves, zoom down a street, and bounce on bumpy roads. At one point, you nearly crash into a truck!

A crash course in car safety

Kids think this ride is a fun way to learn more about cars.

Danielle T. says, "The banks on the curves are incredible. They look really steep. Only ride if you can handle it." Szasha agrees. "People with motion sickness should not ride," she says.

Michael says, "It's a fun, speedy, and scary ride. Lots of kids will like it because they like going fast."

Don't worry—it's safer than it looks. Disney workers tested all the cars first. After all, that's what test driving is all about. You must be at least 40 inches tall to try it.

Millennium Marker

If the Disney Imagineers were making a time capsule to mark Disney's Millennium Celebration, what do you think they would put in it? Some Disney pins? A puppet or a mask? Sure! And they would probably add in some props from Walt Disney World attractions, too.

The words in this puzzle are all names of objects that might go into a Disney Imagineer's time capsule. Use the clues to figure out what the props are. Then use your imagination to think of some others that you would add!

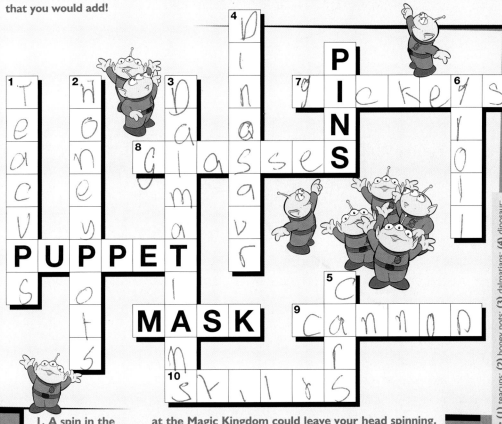

1. A spin in the_____at the Magic Kingdom could leave your head spinning.
2. These jars almost get swept away in Pooh's adventurous ride:_____.
3. You can spot these Disney pups on the Main Street Firehouse:_____.
4. In Countdown to Extinction, your mission is to capture a_____.
5. _____are tested all day long at Test Track.
6. This Norwegian bad guy isn't so bad after all:_____.
7. Doug Funnie wins_____from a radio contest in Disney's Doug Live!
8. Honey, I Shrunk the Audience wouldn't feel as real without_____.
9. A _____booms from the big pirate ship in Pirates of the Caribbean.
10. _____help some Legend of the Lion King performers reach new heights.

WONDERS OF LIFE

You know what you look like on the outside. Now find out what you look like on the inside. This pavilion is all about the human body. It's easy to spend a couple of hours here, so come early to beat the crowds.

Body Wars

Every time you get a cut, it's white blood cells to the rescue. They destroy infections and help you heal. In this attraction, white blood cells mistake a scientist for an infection. She was shrunk for a special mission inside a body—to remove a nasty splinter. Now the white blood cells are after her! Your mission is to rescue her before it's too late.

Go inside a body

This bumpy ride through a human body takes place in a room called a simulator. Together, the simulator and a movie make you feel like you're inside another person. You must be at least 40 inches tall to ride.

74

If the sight of blood makes you woozy, don't ride Body Wars.

Cranium Command

Imagine that you're a pilot. But instead of flying an airplane, you pilot the brain of a 12-year-old boy. That's what happens to Buzzy during this attraction, and you get to go along for the ride.

Buzzy and the brain

The pre-show is a funny cartoon that explains how Buzzy gets his job. Then you go into a theater—and inside the brain with Buzzy. You watch as he tries to get the parts of the brain to work together.

Kids identify with Bobby

The brain in Cranium Command belongs to a boy named Bobby. (The cranium is the part of your skull where your brain is.) It's Buzzy's job to pilot Bobby through a day at school. "I can relate to the things that happen to the boy in the story," says Tate. Can you?

Epcot

HIDDEN MICKEY ALERT! You may spot one in Walt Disney's brain on the "Hall of Brains" poster.

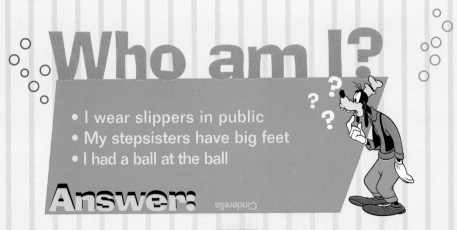

Who am I?

- I wear slippers in public
- My stepsisters have big feet
- I had a ball at the ball

Answer: Cinderella

75

Fitness Fairgrounds

The lobby of the pavilion has so many hands-on activities, the kids think you can spend at least an hour here.

Wonder Cycles are bikes that let you watch a film while riding. The faster you pedal, the faster the action in the film goes!

In the Coach's Corner, a computer checks your tennis, baseball, and golf swings and gives you tips for a better game. In the Sensory Funhouse, the kids enjoy trying to guess what certain objects are without being able to see them. Justin says, "You can touch everything. It's so much fun."

The Making of Me

Where do babies come from? That question and many more are answered in the film *The Making of Me.* The movie is shown in a theater in the middle of the Wonders of Life pavilion. It lasts 14 minutes. It's a good show to watch with your parents.

UNIVERSE OF ENERGY

Discover where energy comes from on this trip through prehistoric times, complete with dinosaurs. The ride is called Ellen's Energy Adventure. It's inside the Universe of Energy pavilion.

Ellen's energy nightmare

The attraction starts with a movie about a woman named Ellen. She is asleep and having a weird dream. She's a contestant on a TV game show—and all of the questions are about energy. Ellen doesn't know much about energy, so she really stinks at the game.

Then Bill Nye, the Science Guy, decides to teach her all about energy. To do it, he takes her (and you) on a trip back in time.

Visit the dinosaurs

First you go into a theater to see another movie. Then the ride part begins. Bill Nye takes you and Ellen to a prehistoric world. You travel through fog and past several types of dinosaurs. Some of them are huge. And they all look real.

At the end of the ride, Ellen gets another chance to play on the TV game show. How does she do this time? That's something you'll have to see for yourself!

Three cheers for energy!

The kids who worked on this book loved Ellen's Energy Adventure. If you like dinosaurs, you'll enjoy it, too. Michael says, "It's an entertaining show. The movies talk about how energy got started, but it's a ride at the same time." Danielle T. thinks "it's neat how the cars split up in the theater. And the Audio-Animatronics dinosaurs and Ellen look real." Szasha says, "The dinosaur part is my favorite. And Ellen is funny."

World Showcase

Anyone can be a world traveler at World Showcase. You can learn about other countries, experience different cultures, and meet people from all over the world. Most of the people who work in each pavilion really come from the country they represent. And they're all happy to talk to you.

The pavilions were built around a lake called World Showcase Lagoon. If you make the trip all the way around the lake, you will walk more than one mile!

CANADA

If you look at a map of North America, Canada is at the top, just above the United States. It's a beautiful country. The Canada pavilion at Epcot is very pretty, too. There's a rocky mountain, a stream, gardens, and a totem pole.

The highlight is a movie called *O Canada!* The scenes completely surround you. Since you stand during the movie, it's easy to turn around and see everything.

What do the kids who worked on this book think about the movie? David B. explains, "It makes you feel like you're moving."

Ashley P. likes "the music and all the information the movie gives you about Canada."

Karyn says, "All the mountains and sledding scenes are beautiful." Nita agrees. "The movie is pretty," she says. "But I don't like standing up. They need seats in that theater!"

Disney added a whole pavilion to Epcot for the Millennium Celebration. It's called the Millennium Village and you'll find it between Canada and the United Kingdom. Lots of different countries are represented there, which means there are all sorts of interesting things to see and do. If you want to learn more, read page 13.

UNITED KINGDOM

From London to the English countryside, this pavilion gives a varied view of the United Kingdom. Some details to look for include the smoke stains painted on the chimneys to make them appear old, and the grassy roofs that are really made of plastic broom bristles. And Tate points out, "There are pretty gardens here."

Lindsay likes "looking at the different stores from the outside."

A group of comedians often performs along World Showcase Promenade near this pavilion. Sometimes, a band plays famous old songs in the garden.

FRANCE

The Eiffel Tower is the best-known landmark at the France pavilion. (The real one is in Paris, France.) The buildings here look just like those in a real French town. Many of the workers here come from France. They speak English with a French accent. Surprise them by saying *bonjour* (pronounced: *bohn-ZHOOR*). It means "good day" in French.

The main attraction—besides the treats at the bakery—is *Impressions de France* (Impressions of France). It's a movie that takes you from one end of France to the other. It's shown on a big screen, and you get to sit down and take in the sights.

Epcot

International Mouse

Mickey is famous all over the world. But not everyone knows the movie-star mouse by that name. In Italy he's called Topolino. In Greece he's known as Miky Maoye. Norwegians call him Mikke Mus. In Sweden he goes by Musse Pigg. And in China he's Mi Lao Shu. That's a lot of names for one mouse to remember!

MOROCCO

The country of Morocco is famous for its mosaics—artwork and patterns that are made up of many tiles. That's why there is beautiful tile work in this pavilion. Moroccan artists made sure the mosaics here were done right.

The buildings are copies of monuments in Moroccan cities, including Fez and Marrakesh. There are lots of shops selling things you would find in Morocco. You can buy baskets, brass, jewelry, or a fez (a type of hat) and other Moroccan clothing.

The Marrakesh restaurant has a belly dancer who entertains in the courtyard, too.

Salam alekoum (pronounced: *sah-LAHM wah-LAY-koom*) means "hello" in Morocco.

JAPAN

The temple out front, called a pagoda, makes the Japanese pavilion easy to spot. It's modeled after a pagoda in the city of Nara, Japan.

Be sure to notice all of the evergreen trees. In Japan, they are symbols of eternal life. Some of the trees found in a traditional Japanese garden will not survive in Florida. So similar trees were used instead.

Japanese drummers often perform outside the pavilion. The huge department store has lots of souvenirs from Japan.

Want to say "good morning" in Japanese? Just say *ohayo gozaimasu* (pronounced: *oh-hi-yoh goh-zy-ee-mahs*).

Just for Kids!

World Showcase has something special to offer kids: Kidcot Funstops. There's one in each country. Here you can make masks and musical instruments to bring to the Tapestry of Nations. Want to know more? Turn to page 13.

THE AMERICAN ADVENTURE

This pavilion is the centerpiece of World Showcase. It's about the United States of America. That's why it's called The American Adventure.

The American Adventure show takes place inside Independence Hall (the real Independence Hall is in Philadelphia, Pennsylvania). The show celebrates the American spirit from the earliest days right up to the present.

Benjamin Franklin and Mark Twain host the show. They look so real, you may forget that they are mechanical. Ben Franklin even walks up stairs!

The American Adventure honors many heroes from history: the Pilgrims, Alexander Graham Bell, Jackie Robinson, Susan B. Anthony, Walt Disney, and more. Historic events are shown on movie screens.

Anna thinks this show is "a perfect way to learn about our heritage. The best part is the movie that reviews many famous Americans."

ITALY

Venice is an Italian city known for waterways called canals. There are no canals at Epcot's Italy, but the pavilion does look a lot like the city. The tower is a smaller version of the Campanile, a famous building in Venice. Notice the gondolas tied to the dock in the lagoon. They are a type of boat used for traveling in the canals of Venice.

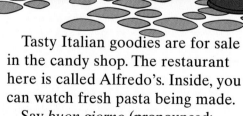

Tasty Italian goodies are for sale in the candy shop. The restaurant here is called Alfredo's. Inside, you can watch fresh pasta being made.

Say *buon giorno* (pronounced: *boo-on JOR-no*). It means "good day" in Italian.

GERMANY

There isn't a village in Germany quite like the one at Epcot. It's a combination of cities and small towns from all around the country. Try to stop by on the hour so you can see the special clock and hear it chime.

Danielle G. says, "The buildings in Germany look authentic. In the center is a beautiful statue on top of a waterfall. I also like the cobblestone pavement." Tate suggests you "try the soft pretzels sold here. There's not much else to do, but it's cool to see how some buildings look in Germany."

In German, "good day" is *guten Tag* (say: *GOOT-en tahkh*).

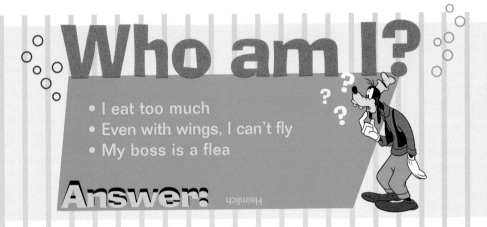

Who am I?

- I eat too much
- Even with wings, I can't fly
- My boss is a flea

Answer: Heimlich

CHINA

Disney's version of the Temple of Heaven is at the center of this pavilion. It's a landmark in the Chinese city of Beijing. Inside, there is a Circle-Vision 360 movie called *Wonders of China: Land of Beauty, Land of Time*. (There are no seats in the theater.)

Before going in to see the movie, take a look at the waiting area. It's decorated in red and gold. These colors mean good luck in China.

The movie is beautiful, but it's a little long. It's more popular with adults than kids.

Karyn prefers the waiting area. "I think the movie is boring. But the exhibit is cool," she says.

To say "hello" in Chinese, say *ni hao* (pronounced: *nee HOW*).

♥**HIDDEN MICKEY ALERT!** Look in the mural above the line for a Viking wearing Mickey Mouse ears.

READER TIP

"Sit in the back of the boat on Maelstrom for the best view."

Sam (age 15)
San Diego, CA

NORWAY

You will discover the history and culture of Norway at this pavilion. (Don't worry about the angry troll. He's harmless.)

The main building is a castle. It was based on an ancient fortress in the capital city of Oslo. Inside, there is a ride called Maelstrom. It's about Norway's history.

He has three heads!

The ride begins in a Viking village. (Vikings were explorers who lived about 1,000 years ago. Many came from Norway.) Next you travel to a forest, where a three-headed troll curses your boat and makes it go backward! After the boat trip, there is a short movie about Norway.

Short but sweet

How do kids feel about Maelstrom? Dawna says, "I like how we sit in a boat like the ones from Norway." David B. wishes the ride were longer. "I still think it's the best thing in World Showcase, even though it's so short."

Saying "hello" is easy here. It's *god dag* (say: *goo DAHG*).

Go to Maelstrom late in the day, when the line is shorter.

Epcot

MEXICO

The pyramid-shaped building at the Mexico pavilion is home to El Río del Tiempo: The River of Time. This is a slow boat trip through scenes of Mexican life.

Film clips show cliff divers in Acapulco, speed boats in Manzanillo, and beautiful sea creatures in Isla Mujeres. You see many colorful displays showing Mexican traditions. At the end of the boat ride, you can visit several shops with Mexican crafts, sombreros, and colorful blankets.

Brad thinks "the boat ride is fun. There are so many things to look at." Dawna likes "the paintings, because I think Mexican art is really neat." David G. thinks the ride "is a nice way to learn Mexico's history."

"Hello" here is *hola* (say: *OH-lah*).

Entertainment

E pcot is Millennium central. That means that there is more entertainment here than ever. There are lots of shows and special performances every day of the year. For more information, check a park guidemap.

ILLUMINATIONS 2000— REFLECTIONS OF EARTH

An amazing fireworks show takes place each night on and around World Showcase Lagoon. It's a special Millennium show. You can get a good view of it from anywhere around the lagoon.

JAMMITORS

One of the loudest and wildest shows is inside Future World, where musicians bang out rhythms on trash cans and, sometimes, on each other. Szasha says, "They're fun and funny."

TAPESTRY OF NATIONS

Join in the fun during this festive show at World Showcase. The action happens all around you. Fancy puppets and performers wearing unusual costumes and masks dance, sing, and make music with you.

WORLD SHOWCASE PERFORMERS

There is some form of entertainment at each of the pavilions in World Showcase. A couple of the highlights include The Living Statues in France and the British Invasion in the United Kingdom. The Living Statues are people dressed as statues. They look like they are made of stone, but then they surprise you by moving! The British Invasion is a funky band that sounds like The Beatles.

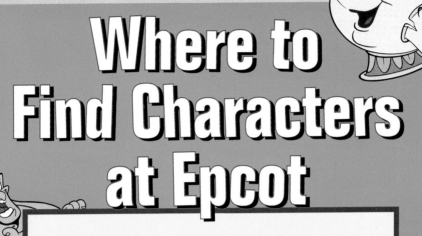

Where to Find Characters at Epcot

Mickey and his pals often appear at the **MouseGear** shop. Sport Goofy can sometimes be spotted at the **Wonders of Life** pavilion.

In World Showcase, you can greet Mickey and his closest friends at **The American Adventure**. You might find Belle and the Beast near **France**, Jasmine and Aladdin in **Morocco**, and Snow White in **Germany**. But the best spot for character sightings is the **United Kingdom**. Alice, Peter Pan, Mary Poppins, and Winnie the Pooh can usually be seen here during the day. Check a park guidemap or ask a cast member for times. And don't forget to ask the characters to autograph page 160 of this book!

Start your day early at Test Track. Then go to the Wonders of Life pavilion to ride Body Wars and see Cranium Command. If there's time before lunch, see all of the attractions in the new Imagination! pavilion.

Remember: World Showcase doesn't open until 11 A.M.

Need a refreshing splash? Visit Cool Wash by Test Track, the squirting sidewalk that leads to World Showcase, or the fountain by Wonders of Life.

Check the electronic Tip Board in Millennium Central. It lets you know how long the wait is for many attractions.

There is a special garbage can in the Electric Umbrella restaurant and a special drinking fountain near the Fountain of Nations. Why are they special? They talk!

Bring pins with you so you'll have something to trade with other guests during the Millennium Celebration. (Be sure to get a parent's permission before you trade anything.)

Buy a passport at any World Showcase shop and get it stamped in every country. It's a great reminder of your trip.

Try not to squeeze the movies at Canada, France, and China all into one day.

Take time to talk to the people who work in World Showcase. Most of them come from the country of the pavilion they represent, and they have many interesting stories to tell.

It might be difficult to walk around World Showcase during the Tapestry of Nations show.

Attraction Ratings

COOL
(Check It Out)

- Food Rocks
- China
- Italy
- United Kingdom
- Mexico
- Germany
- Japan

REALLY COOL
(Don't Miss)

- The Living Seas
- The Circle of Life
- The American Adventure
- Journey Into Your Imagination
- Spaceship Earth
- Mexico boat ride
- France
- Canada
- Morocco

THE COOLEST
(See at Least Twice)

- Test Track
- Body Wars
- Cranium Command
- Innoventions
- Universe of Energy
- Honey, I Shrunk the Audience
- Norway
- Living with the Land
- Millennium Village

Your favorite Epcot attractions

Disney-MGM Studios

The Disney-MGM Studios lets you see some of the magic of making movies and TV shows. There are attractions that show how animation is done, how sound effects are made, how stunts are performed, and lots more.

The park looks a little like Hollywood did back in the 1940s. Hollywood is the California city where movie-making got its big start. The Disney-MGM Studios got its big start in 1989. Since then lots of famous movies and TV shows have been made there. A crew might even be filming something when you are visiting.

One of the best things about this park is that you can be a part of some attractions. It's fun to be right in the middle of the action, so be sure to volunteer. You will also get to meet a ton of characters, including the stars of some of Disney's recent animated hits—so be sure to have your autograph book handy.

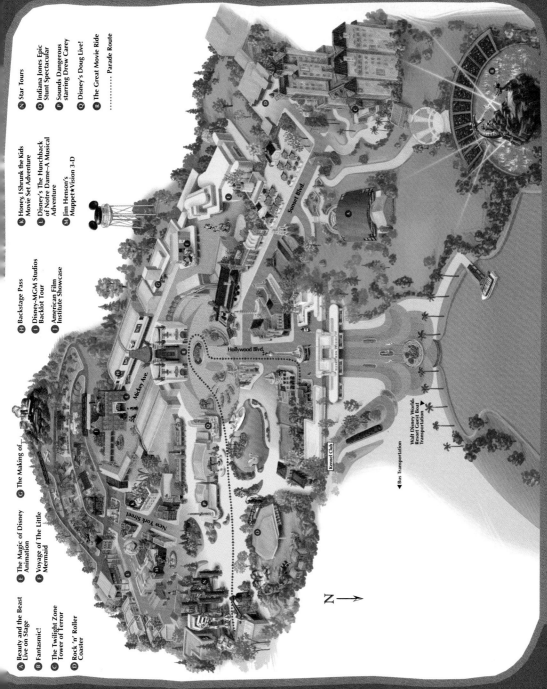

A Beauty and the Beast Live on Stage
B Fantasmic!
C The Twilight Zone Tower of Terror
D Rock 'n' Roller Coaster

E The Magic of Disney Animation
F Voyage of The Little Mermaid

G The Making of...

H Backstage Pass
I Disney-MGM Studios Backlot Tour
J American Film Institute Showcase

K Honey, I Shrunk the Kids Movie Set Adventure
L Disney's The Hunchback of Notre Dame–A Musical Adventure
M Jim Henson's Muppet★Vision 3-D

N Star Tours
O Indiana Jones Epic Stunt Spectacular
P Sounds Dangerous starring Drew Carey
Q Disney's Doug Live!
R The Great Movie Ride
.... Parade Route

Sunset Blvd.

Hollywood Blvd.

Mickey Ave.

New York Street

Kennel Club

▼Bus Transportation

Walt Disney World Resort Guest Boat Transportation ▶

N →

Use this map to explore the Disney-MGM Studios theme park.

❤**HIDDEN MICKEY ALERT!** You might be standing on the biggest Hidden Mickey in this theme park and not even know it. See if you can find it on the map on page 91.

LINE GAMES The ghost of a pianist counts the beats on these old and spirited music sheets. Can you find them?

SCARY Attraction Reaction

ROUGH Attraction Reaction

DARK Attraction Reaction

Disney-MGM Studios

The Twilight Zone Tower of Terror

Tower of Terror is the tallest attraction at Walt Disney World. For some people, it's also the scariest.

Legend says that one Halloween night, lightning hit The Hollywood Tower Hotel. A whole section of the hotel disappeared! So did an elevator carrying five people. No one ever saw them again.

Now the hotel is haunted. If you dare to enter it, you are in for a few surprises. First, you walk through the dusty hotel lobby. Then you enter a tiny room, where Rod Serling appears on TV. (He was the star of a sometimes scary show called *The Twilight Zone*.) Once Rod tells the story of The Hollywood Tower Hotel, get ready—you are on your way to the Twilight Zone.

Going down!

After waiting in the boiler room for a little while, you are given a seat in a big elevator. The elevator ride takes you on a short tour of the hotel, where you see many special effects. But the highlight comes when the elevator cables snap. Whooosh! You plunge eight stories! Next the elevator shoots up to the hotel's 13th floor. It teeters for a moment and then . . . it drops again and again at blazing speed!

A thrilling experience

People who love thrills think this is a great ride. David G. says, "Get ready because you plunge more than three times. Tower of Terror really lives up to its motto: Fear every drop!"

You must be at least 40 inches tall to ride—and very brave!

This ride is indoors, so you can't see the track before getting in line. There is a chicken exit if you change your mind.

Disney-MGM Studios

Rock 'n' Roller Coaster

This ride really rocks! It travels at top speeds and flips you upside down three times. It also has a rock 'n' roll sound track that will have you dancing in your seat.

Rock 'n' Roller Coaster goes really fast—it takes you from zero to 60 miles per hour in the first three seconds of the ride! You need the speed because you're on your way to a party at an Aerosmith concert—and you're running late.

The ride takes place in a limousine on a roller coaster track. The track looks like a road in California. (You travel on the road to get to the concert.) The limousine's radio is tuned to the concert. You can hear the band is about to begin, but you're not moving yet. Then, just as the concert starts, the light turns green and you're on your way. Hang on!

Ask a cast member if you are tall enough to take this wild ride.

Beauty and the Beast Live on Stage

I t's hard to keep quiet during this stage show—it makes you want to clap and sing along. The music comes straight from the Disney film *Beauty and the Beast.*

The story is the same, but the order of the songs is different. (A few songs are left out, too.)

Be their guest

The show starts with "Be Our Guest." It's a colorful musical number—just like in the movie. Then the show goes back to the beginning, where Belle is dreaming of faraway places. Soon, she is a prisoner in the Beast's castle. Lumière, Cogsworth, Mrs. Potts, and the rest of the gang are there to help. In the end, the spell is broken. The Beast becomes human again!

A real kid pleaser

Taran says, "If you love the movie, you'll like this show."

"I love when the white doves fly out at the end," says Nita. "I also love the costumes and the music." Karyn enjoys this show, too. "There are so many great details, like the dancing dishes and spoons," she says.

The show is performed several times each day. Read a park guidemap for exact times. (You can get a free map at any shop in the Disney-MGM Studios. Just ask!)

The sidewalk by The Great Movie Ride is covered with handprints and footprints. They belong to famous stars. Put your palms and feet in the prints and compare your prints with theirs.

The Great Movie Ride

How many movies have you seen in your lifetime? Hundreds? Thousands? Well, how many have you actually been in? Probably not too many! This attraction lets you ride through scenes from old movies.

Pay attention!

First, you'll watch short clips from famous films. Pay close attention—these are the scenes that you will visit later on.

As you enter the ride vehicle, take time to look around. The room is set up like a movie set (a stage where movie scenes are filmed). The background looks like the hills of Hollywood. That's the California town where movie-making got its big start.

A trip to Munchkinland

Once the car starts moving, you'll pass through scenes from movies like *Mary Poppins*, *Alien*, and *Fantasia*. One of the best scenes is straight out of the *Wizard of Oz*. It looks just like Munchkinland! (Beware: The Wicked Witch of the West pops in for a visit.)

You may also get caught in a shootout and come close to being slimed by an alien. The ride ends with a movie that shows more clips from great films.

What do kids think about The Great Movie Ride? "It's really cool," says Robert, "but it could have more action in it." Karyn disagrees. "No matter how many times I ride, I still love it."

♥HIDDEN MICKEY ALERT! Mickey and pals are drawn onto the Well of Souls. Look for them during the Indiana Jones scene.

HOT  TIP

The animators don't work on the weekends. If you want to watch them, visit during the week.

The Magic of Disney Animation

Anybody can create a cartoon character. All you need is a pencil, some paper, and a little imagination. But how do you get that character to *move*? That's where the animation part comes in.

Learn how it's done

This attraction shows you how *Mulan*, *Fantasia 2000*, *Tarzan*, and other movies were made. It also gives you a chance to watch artists at work on one of Disney's upcoming animated films.

In the waiting area, there are drawings on the walls. Later, you'll find out how artists called *animators* bring these kinds of sketches to life.

Spy on the animators

Toward the beginning of the tour, you get to meet a real Disney artist. There's even time for you to ask questions.

Next, you walk through a studio. It's where many animators work. (They are behind glass walls, so you can see them.) Your tour guide will explain the animation process as you watch. That way you'll understand what the animators are doing.

It takes about 35 minutes to see everything. Try to go early in the day, when the animators are busy working. They usually go home at about 5 o'clock.

Disney-MGM Studios

You Be the Animator

Once the animator has outlined a drawing on a cel in ink, it's the painter's job to add color. The painter always uses a color chart to figure out which colors to pick. That way Tigger's tummy isn't yellow in one scene and orange in the next!

Use crayons or colored pencils and the color chart below to take Tigger and his friend from black and white to the wonderful world of color.

| 1 | 2 | 3 | 4 | 5 | 6 |

HOT **TIP!** For the best view at Voyage of The Little Mermaid, sit toward the back of the theater.

Voyage of The Little Mermaid

SCARY Attraction Reaction

LOUD Attraction Reaction

DARK Attraction Reaction

You don't have to be a fish to have fun underwater—and this show proves it. In it, you go below the ocean's surface with Ariel and her friends from *The Little Mermaid*. They sing and act out the story on stage. Ariel and Eric are played by actors. Flounder, Sebastian, and other creatures are puppets.

Under the sea

There are some great special effects that draw you into the show. A screen of water makes it seem like the theater really is under the sea. Lasers flash, lightning strikes, and mist sprays the audience. Scenes from the movie are shown on a big screen behind the stage.

A winning combination

Dawna thinks "the combination of actors, puppets, movie clips, lasers, bubbles, and water all add up to a great show."

Lindsay agrees. "This is a totally creative show. You feel like you're under the water, especially when you get a little wet with the mist."

Tate thinks they leave out too much. "Even though most people know what happens, it would be better to have more scenes," he says.

98

HIDDEN MICKEY ALERT! Lasers at the start of the show form a Mickey head.

Who am I?

- I like spaghetti
- I don't have a home
- My girlfriend is a cocker spaniel

Answer: Tramp

The Making of...

If you have ever wondered what goes into "the making of" a Disney movie, then head to this attraction. It goes behind the scenes and lets you in on some Hollywood secrets. You might hear from actors, directors, or other people whose jobs are listed in movie credits.

The attraction changes every so often and might not be open during your visit. Ashley J. thinks "probably grown-ups would like it more. If you are on a tight schedule, then maybe you shouldn't go to this one. But I learned a lot of things I didn't know about making movies."

HOT TIP!

You can sing in the rain under a special umbrella on New York Street.

HOT  TIP

Ask a cast member or check a guidemap to find out if a TV show or movie is being filmed during your visit.

Backstage Pass

Do you know what you want to be when you grow up? An actor? How about a movie director? In either case, this is the attraction for you. Here you'll get a chance to see how these jobs are done. The tour shows how scenes from live-action movies and television shows were created.

Tricks of the trade

Backstage Pass teaches you lots of movie-making tricks. You might see how film shot in front of a plain blue screen can be combined with almost any background. You'll also find out how sets are created.

Lights! Camera! Action!

"I've never been on a tour that took me backstage like that," says Michael. "We got to see actual props from a movie." You might even be able to see a real scene from a movie or a television show being filmed. If a crew is filming when you visit, you can watch the action happen on one of the attraction's soundstages.

Disney-MGM Studios Backlot Tour

There's a real working studio at this theme park. A tram ride lets you see parts of the backstage areas where movies and TV shows are filmed. You also see how a battle scene at sea is shot.

A grand canyon

The trip includes a stop at Catastrophe Canyon—a special effects area. Here you see a fire and a flash flood. The tram also takes you through the costume and lighting departments, and past props from famous movies.

"I like Catastrophe Canyon," says Lissy. "It shows that special effects are safer than they look."

Robert agrees. "Catastrophe Canyon is really cool. When the explosions go off, it gets really hot. Then when the water comes down, it gets really cold."

Where's the back door?

Ashley P. enjoys touring the streets and "seeing the houses without the backs. They only film the fronts for the television shows, so that's all they build," she points out.

Nita has seen this attraction before. "I like this tour," she says, "but a lot depends on the guide. If you get a really good guide, the tour is much better."

Honey, I Shrunk the Kids Movie Set Adventure

The backyard from the *Honey, I Shrunk the Kids* movie has been re-created as a big playground. Even grown-ups feel small here. There are 30-foot blades of grass, huge Lego toys, a giant ant, and more. There are things to climb on, slide down, and explore.

"It looks more like *Honey, I Blew Up the Garden*!" says Taran. "I like the cave the best."

Lissy thinks "the whole place is really neat. Not just the slides and the swings—there's a lot for older kids to notice. Everything looks like it comes straight from the movie."

Most kids enjoy getting wet under the leaky hose. Water squirts from a different spot each time.

"I like the slides and the big net, but I think it's more for younger kids," says Brian L.

Karyn agrees. "I'm the type of person who would just love to take younger kids around and watch them have fun."

HOT There's a big map at the entrance to Honey, I Shrunk the Kids Movie Set Adventure. Use it! **TIP**

Disney-MGM Studios

Jim Henson's Muppet*Vision 3-D

Don't miss this attraction—it's one of Walt Disney World's best. It begins with a funny pre-show starring Fozzie Bear, Gonzo, Scooter, and Sam Eagle. Then you go into a special theater that looks just like the one from the old *Muppet Show*. Here, you see 3-D movie effects mixed with some other special effects. It's hard to tell what's part of the movie and what's real.

Amazing effects

"The characters come right out at you," says Lissy. "It's cool that they have real things happening, so when they throw a pie you think it will be real." Adam W. enjoys the show. "My favorite parts are the squirting water and when the screen blows up. You feel like you're going to get hit."

Kirsti is a Muppet fan, too. "This is my favorite show and it always will be," she says. Taran thinks "it's awesome. I also love the little 3-D character, Waldo, because he seems like he's talking only to you." (Waldo is a special character that was dreamed up just for this show.)

Look around the theater

Nita says to look at the back of the theater "because a lot happens back there and most people miss it."

Karyn says, "You have to see this movie a few times to get all the jokes and appreciate more of the details, like the two guys sitting in the balcony. They're really funny."

Star Tours

Soar through the galaxy on an out-of-control spaceship and experience the thrills of the movie *Star Wars*. Your pilot is Captain Rex. He's new on the job and can't seem to find his way through all the giant ice crystals and other spaceships.

It feels real

This ride takes place on a flight simulator, the same type used to train astronauts and pilots. The combination of the simulator and the movie makes you feel like you're really rocketing through outer space.

Rex is a rotten pilot

Brad says, "The pilot makes the ride really fun. He keeps going the wrong way." Robert thinks "it's really neat. It's funny when the pilot can't find the brakes. If you know what the movie *Star Wars* is like, you'll really like this ride."

Danielle G. agrees. "It feels and looks like you're really traveling through space." Dawna adds, "It seems like you're going really fast even though you're not going anywhere."

You must be at least 40 inches tall to ride.

Disney's Doug Live!

Everybody's favorite boy from 21 Jumbo Street comes to life in this entertaining musical show. All of the characters are played by humans—even Porkchop, Doug's trusty pup. But the actors usually look and sound a lot like the cartoon characters, so they are easy enough to recognize.

Name that tune

Doug wins a radio contest by identifying a silly song and the prize is two tickets to The Beets concert. He wants to go with Patti, his favorite girl in the whole world. But Roger asks her first.

Quailman to the rescue!

Doug is feeling very bad about himself. But his alter-ego Quailman tells him all he has to do is be himself, and Patti will like him. As it turns out, he's right.

During the concert, some of the action happens right in the audience. David G. advises: "Sit in the front and Doug and Skeeter will sit right by you to watch The Beets. It makes you feel like you're in the show."

Some guests really *are* in the show. Jennifer says, "Being Quailkid would make the experience even more special. If you're not picked, ask a parent to volunteer to play a Beet."

HIDDEN MICKEY ALERT! Some of the stars on the wall behind the pizza counter form a Mickey head.

Toy Story Pizza Planet Arcade

This arcade and restaurant looks a lot like Andy's favorite pizza place from the movie *Toy Story*. It's located near Jim Henson's Muppet*Vision 3-D. If you have trouble finding it, just look for the giant Mr. Potato Head and Rex the dinosaur sitting on top of the building. Inside are lots of "claw" prize machines and video games, plus a fast-food counter with pizza, salad, and juice boxes. Brian F. says, "I like it because it's just like the movie."

Disney's The Hunchback of Notre Dame—A Musical Adventure

You are invited to the Festival of Fools. The celebration is packed with dancers and puppets, all in colorful costumes.

This live show is based on Disney's animated film *The Hunchback of Notre Dame.* If you've seen the movie, you'll know the characters. The storyteller is Clopin, King of the Gypsies. He gets lots of help from his band of gypsy players, who sing, dance, and act out the tale. Judge Frollo, Esmeralda, and Phoebus also make appearances. And those wacky gargoyles, Victor, Hugo, and Laverne are there to make everybody laugh.

Szasha says, "I think it's a cool play, even though I haven't seen the movie. I like the puppets and live actors. Quasimodo rings the bells by pulling a rope, and they really work." Danielle T. likes "how the actors go into the audience. Their costumes are great."

Indiana Jones Epic Stunt Spectacular

LOUD
Attraction Reaction

Fire, explosions, daring escapes, and other special effects are the stars of this attraction. Stunt men and women act out scenes from the movie *Raiders of the Lost Ark* and show how special effects are done. The audience watches from a large theater, and several adults are chosen to perform with the pros. (It's too dangerous for kids.)

Fun for everyone

"I love this show. I think it's great for all ages," says Karyn. One of the best parts of the show is the scene where the giant ball rolls down and seems to crush Indiana Jones. "I was at the edge of my seat!" says Brian L.

Don't try this at home

Lissy says the music adds to the suspense and "the stunt people are just fantastic." Brian L. views it as pure excitement: "I love how they were falling from the towers, and then they were always okay."

You learn a lot about movie stunts at this show. "They explain everything they do, making it even more fun to watch," says Karyn.

After the show, visit the area by the exit called Sound Works, for some do-it-yourself sound effects.

Sounds Dangerous starring Drew Carey

You may have seen a 3-D movie before, but have you ever seen a movie with 3-D sound? For this one you wear special headphones that make the action sound like it's happening all around you.

Inspector Carey

Drew Carey is the hero of this funny movie. He's supposed to be an actor whose character is an undercover detective. But the detective is not very good at his job. And he's wearing a camera, so the audience can see (and hear) all the mistakes he makes.

Lights out!

Drew sneaks into a warehouse to spy on some jewel smugglers. When he runs into a security guard, he panics—and hides the camera in his mouth (which breaks it, of course).

The next thing you know the theater is dark and you can only hear what's going on through your headphones. The sounds seem so real that the action is easy to follow.

Before catching up with the bad guys, Drew ends up on some silly adventures. Keep an ear out for bees, elephants, race cars, and a few more surprises along the way.

Rascal Round-Up

What's scarier than one of Disney's meanest bad guys? Thirteen of them! The villains have escaped from their movies and are hiding in this puzzle. Their names are written forward, backward, across, diagonally, up, and down. Use a pencil to catch these meanies before they get away.

Scar
Hades
Frollo
Shere Kahn
Gaston
Hopper
Jafar
Sid
Ursula
Hook
Shan-Yu
Maleficent
Cruella

T	N	E	C	I	F	E	L	A	M
S	H	E	R	U	K	S	I	D	N
G	D	A	R	S	J	A	C	U	H
A	K	O	U	E	K	A	Y	K	A
S	L	L	O	H	P	N	H	O	K
T	A	L	O	D	A	P	O	O	E
O	J	O	E	H	N	D	O	H	R
N	U	R	S	U	L	A	E	H	E
Y	A	F	R	O	R	A	C	S	H
U	R	A	F	A	J	C	A	I	S

Entertainment

Lights! Camera! Action! There's a lot of star-studded entertainment at the Disney-MGM Studios. Most of it has a TV or movie theme. Two of the best shows are described below.

FANTASMIC!

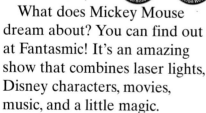

What does Mickey Mouse dream about? You can find out at Fantasmic! It's an amazing show that combines laser lights, Disney characters, movies, music, and a little magic.

Mickey's dreams are fun to watch—but some of them are a little scary. (Disney villains keep turning his dreams into nightmares.) In the end, good wins over evil and Mickey's dreams are happy once more.

Fantasmic! is presented in a theater behind The Twilight Zone Tower of Terror attraction. It's very popular, so be sure to line up at least 45 minutes before the show starts. And, if it isn't summer, bring a jacket or a sweater—it can get chilly!

MULAN PARADE

The star of *Mulan* marches in a parade on Hollywood Boulevard every afternoon. Look for fancy floats, brave soldiers, and giant puppets, plus the Matchmaker, Shang, the villain Shan-Yu on a giant bed of skulls, and Mulan's trusty sidekick, Mushu the dragon.

Where to Find Characters at Disney-MGM Studios

There are lots of places to meet Disney characters at the Studios. One of the best spots is **Mickey Avenue**. Disney characters stop by all day. Go late in the afternoon when there aren't as many people, and you can get a ton of pictures. If you check a park guidemap or ask a cast member, you can find the times that characters are scheduled to appear.

You won't find Mickey on Mickey Avenue. He's in **Animation Courtyard** posing for pictures and signing autographs all day long. Stop by and say hello!

If you want to pose with the characters over breakfast or lunch, have a meal at the **Hollywood & Vine** restaurant. Be sure to ask each character to sign page 160 of this book.

DISNEY-MGM STUDIOS TIPS

Arrive at the Disney-MGM Studios before the opening time. The gates usually open about a half hour before the scheduled time.

The character breakfast at the Hollywood & Vine restaurant is a great way to start the day.

There is one "chicken exit" at Tower of Terror, right before you get on the ride elevator, just in case you change your mind at the last minute.

Check the Tip Board on Hollywood Boulevard. It tells you which attractions have the shortest lines and when the next shows start.

Some stage shows don't open until late morning. Be sure to check your guidemap for exact showtimes.

To get a good spot to see the afternoon parade, line up on Hollywood Boulevard about 30 minutes early.

Mickey Avenue is the best place to meet Disney characters.

The front rows at Fantasmic! get wet. The best seats are in the back at either end of the theater.

See Jim Henson's Muppet*Vision 3-D, Voyage of The Little Mermaid, and Star Tours in the morning before the lines get too long.

Attraction Ratings

COOL
(Check It Out)

- The Great Movie Ride
- Backstage Pass
- Disney's The Hunchback of Notre Dame—A Musical Adventure
- The Making of…

REALLY COOL
(Don't Miss)

- Indiana Jones Epic Stunt Spectacular
- Disney-MGM Studios Backlot Tour
- Honey, I Shrunk the Kids Movie Set Adventure
- Disney's Doug Live!
- Fantasmic!

THE COOLEST
(See at Least Twice)

- Jim Henson's Muppet*Vision 3-D
- Star Tours
- Tower of Terror
- Beauty and the Beast Live on Stage
- The Magic of Disney Animation
- Voyage of The Little Mermaid
- Sounds Dangerous starring Drew Carey
- Rock 'n' Roller Coaster

Disney-MGM Studios

Your favorite Disney-MGM Studios attractions

Tower of Terror
Rock 'n' Roller Coaster
Sounds Danger

Disney's Animal Kingdom

The newest park in Walt Disney World is called Animal Kingdom. It celebrates animals of every kind, from lions, tigers, and zebras to giant turtles whose ancestors lived during the time of the dinosaurs. And they're all real! You may get closer to them than you've ever been before. There are dinosaurs, too. The dinos aren't real, but they sure seem it.

Animal Kingdom is a huge theme park with many attractions. Five Magic Kingdoms could fit inside it. Just like at the Magic Kingdom, there are different "lands" to visit in Animal Kingdom. The major lands are Safari Village, DinoLand U.S.A., Asia, Africa, and Camp Minnie-Mickey.

You enter the park through The Oasis. It's a big garden with plants and animals. Take some time to look around. Then cross a bridge to Safari Village and decide which land to explore first.

114

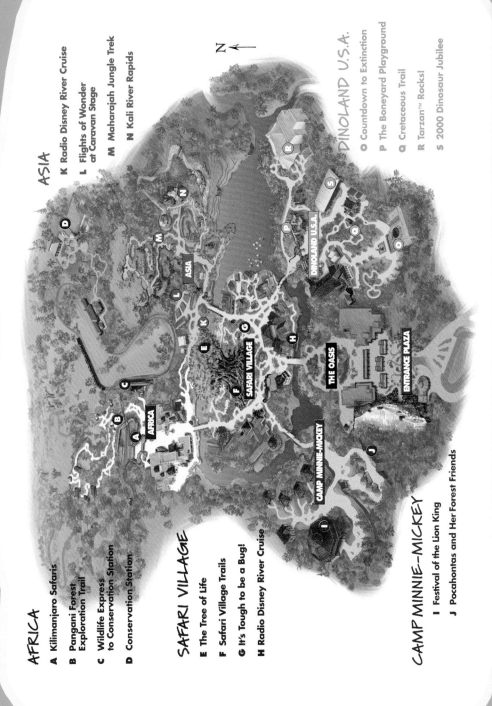

AFRICA

A Kilimanjaro Safaris

B Pangani Forest Exploration Trail

C Wildlife Express to Conservation Station

D Conservation Station

SAFARI VILLAGE

E The Tree of Life

F Safari Village Trails

G It's Tough to be a Bug!

H Radio Disney River Cruise

CAMP MINNIE–MICKEY

I Festival of the Lion King

J Pocahontas and Her Forest Friends

ASIA

K Radio Disney River Cruise

L Flights of Wonder at Caravan Stage

M Maharajah Jungle Trek

N Kali River Rapids

DINOLAND U.S.A.

O Countdown to Extinction

P The Boneyard Playground

Q Cretaceous Trail

R Tarzan™ Rocks!

S 2000 Dinosaur Jubilee

What's the best way to see Animal Kingdom? Use this map to help you decide!

115

Safari Village

Safari Village is the island gateway to all the other lands in the park. The Tree of Life stands near the center of Safari Village. If you wander about its roots you'll see all kinds of animals.

The Tree of Life

This man-made tree is 145 feet tall. From far away it looks like any other tree. When you get up close, you'll realize that this is not an ordinary tree. It's covered with animals!

Artists have carved 325 animal images into its trunk. In fact, it's called The Tree of Life because it's covered with so many different kinds of animal life.

Jennifer says, "It's a must-see. Although I guess it's fairly hard to miss a 14-story-tall tree!" she adds. Grace has a tip: "The best place to get a close look at the animals carved into the tree is while waiting in line for It's Tough to be a Bug!"

♥**HIDDEN MICKEY ALERT!** There's a mouse in the moss! Look for clusters of moss near the tiger. They form a Hidden Mickey.

If you hate creepy crawlers, skip It's Tough to be a Bug!

LINE GAMES

This orphan ant, who wears a red dress, says, "The sun'll come out." Which bug do you guess? (Hint: She's on a poster.)

It's Tough to be a Bug!

The Tree of Life has a hollow trunk. It's cool, dark, and roomy inside. That makes it a great place to watch a 3-D movie called It's Tough to be a Bug! It's hosted by Flik, the star of *A Bug's Life*.

This movie is about the tiny creatures that outnumber all others on our planet—bugs. In it, animated insects use music and special effects to show how hard their lives are.

Most of the bugs are friendly and funny. But when Flik's enemy Hopper makes an appearance, the show gets a little bit scary. Hopper wants to exterminate *you*!

Kids love this exciting show. As Jennifer says, "The effects make it seem so real!" David G. agrees. "Watch out for the stink bug," he warns. "And lean forward if you don't want to get stung!" Grace adds.

Disney's Animal Kingdom

Radio Disney River Cruise

Flik and Hopper aren't the only famous animals hanging out in The Tree of Life. There are a couple of humans you might recognize, too. Who are they? None other than Mark and Zippy from the "Just Plain Mark and Zippy Show" on Radio Disney. As usual, you can't see them, but you can certainly hear them.

These funny fellows have recorded a special show that is broadcast from the top of the tree, and the only place to listen to it is aboard the Radio Disney River Cruise. This boat ride is sure to have you dancing in your seat. The trip is filled with music and fun facts about all sorts of animals. You can get on in Safari Village or Asia. It's also a great way to see what there is to do at Animal Kingdom.

DinoLand U.S.A.

The entrance to this land is marked by a giant dinosaur skeleton. Inside, you will find life-like dinosaurs as well as live animals that have existed since prehistoric times. The main attraction is Countdown to Extinction, but there are lots of other things to see and do. For a hand-clapping good time, watch Tarzan Rocks! at the Theater in the Wild. In DinoLand you can also dig for bones in an amazing playground, learn about real dinosaurs, or spend some quiet time on a short nature trail.

READER TIP

"Countdown to Extinction is very loud and dark, and it really jerks and pulls you around. Some young kids won't like it at all!"
Julia (age 1?)
Prairieville, L

Countdown to Extinction

SCARY Attraction Reaction

DARK Attraction Reaction

LOUD Attraction Reaction

ROUGH Attraction Reaction

This thrilling ride takes you back to the last few minutes of the Cretaceous Period. (That's when the dinosaurs died out.)

Save the dinosaur

At Countdown to Extinction, your job is to save the last iguanodon. You have to brave a meteor shower and the largest Audio-Animatronics creature Disney has ever made. It's a dinosaur called a carnotaurus, and it may be the ugliest thing you've ever seen. This monster has the face of a toad, horns like a bull, and squirrel-like arms. It looks like it's alive. The nostrils even move as it breathes. And, boy, can

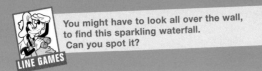

You might have to look all over the wall, to find this sparkling waterfall. Can you spot it?

LINE GAMES

it run. The carnotaurus runs for about 30 feet. Be careful! This hungry monster is not just after the iguanodon—it wants to eat *you*, too.

An exciting (and scary) ride

The kids agree that this is a very exciting ride, but one that might not be for everyone. "This is one of the most thrilling rides," says David G., "but it might be way too scary for some kids." Grace feels the same way. "It's bumpy and the dinosaurs seem so real. That's what makes it so much fun," she adds. Jennifer loves the scary factor. "This is one of the best rides I've ever been on!" she says. (Kids who don't like scary rides can find some quieter dino encounters at the 2000 Dinosaur Jubilee.)

You must be at least 48 inches tall to ride Countdown to Extinction.

Cretaceous Trail

For a real "live" treat, walk down the Cretaceous Trail. This short path is filled with plants and animals that have been around longer than people have. Their ancestors lived with dinosaurs! Be on the lookout for birds and alligators and other ancient beasts.

The trail is a peaceful way to pass some time after riding Countdown to Extinction—or if you are waiting while others ride.

2000 Dinosaur Jubilee

Have you ever seen a tooth that's bigger than your hand? It probably belonged to somebody pretty ferocious. The ones on display here certainly did!

The 2000 Dinosaur Jubilee is a huge tent filled with copies of real dinosaur skeletons. You'll see skeletons of some dinosaurs you've probably heard about, and others you may never have even imagined before. Like the *Archelon Ischyros*, which looks like a gigantic turtle— it's probably taller than you are!

There are also many displays here that are interesting even if you don't know much about dinosaurs. (Look for the Claw & Teeth exhibit.) And there are lots of benches, so it's a great place to relax and cool off.

Disney's Animal Kingdom

The Boneyard Playground

Are you ready to dive into the biggest sandbox you've ever seen? It's here and it's filled with bones! You can uncover the bones of a mammoth and find clues about how the animal died.

There are also dinosaur footprints that roar when you jump in them, and a xylophone that's made of dinosaur bones. There's a rope maze for climbing and plenty of slippery slides, too. Be sure to check out the OldenGate Bridge. It's made from a huge dinosaur skeleton.

Kids have a fun time exploring the Boneyard. David G. says, "You really feel like you're an archeologist searching for bones and fossils."

HOT TIP

The xylophone is next to the truck in The Boneyard Playground. Press the bones to make music.

Tarzan™ Rocks!

LOUD Attraction Reaction

The stars of this energetic musical show can't stay still. And you won't be able to, either. As soon as it starts you'll be tapping your toes and dancing in your seat to music from the movie *Tarzan*.

Rock and roll show

The band is rocking and the performers are rolling—literally! They're wearing in-line skates instead of shoes. Even on wheels they can dance and jump, and do all sorts of tricks in the air.

From tree to swaying tree

Lots of the characters in the show wear in-line skates, but Tarzan doesn't. Actually, he doesn't wear shoes at all—that would make it much harder for him to climb tall trees! And he does plenty of tree climbing in this stage show. He even swings from a couple of branches. Does Jane come along for the ride? Of course! Would *you* pass up an opportunity like that?

Africa

What African words can you spot on line?
Try finding TWIGA (giraffe). Hint: It's on a sign.

LINE GAMES

Before creating this land, Disney Imagineers spent months on the continent of Africa learning all about the plants and animals there. When they came back, they made an African forest and a grassland in Florida. Then they filled it with hundreds of the same animals they had seen in Africa. Most of the animals in Animal Kingdom came from special parks and zoos around the world. You can see many animals on a safari ride and learn all about them at Conservation Station.

Kilimanjaro Safaris

In this wild jungle adventure, you ride in a vehicle that's wide open. There's almost nothing between you and the animals! You may see hippos, lions, giraffes, rhinos, elephants, and more. Some animals may even come up close. But don't worry—the dangerous animals can't get near you.

After a calm sight-seeing tour, the ride takes a different twist. There are poachers hunting for elephants, and the animals need your help. The ride ends with a wild chase over muddy roads to catch the bad guys. Eric says, "Chasing the poachers isn't scary. But driving over the broken bridge is!"

Kids love the Kilimanjaro Safaris. It's Grace's favorite ride in Animal Kingdom. "I've never been so close to animals like that before," she says. "Some of them even came right up to our jeep!" Jennifer adds.

Pangani Forest Exploration Trail

After you take a ride on the Kilimanjaro Safaris, go for a walk on the Pangani Forest Exploration Trail. This nature trail is filled with many exciting sights. You'll come nose-to-nose with a naked mole rat and look for hippos underwater. Exotic fish and birds live in the African Aviary.

No binoculars necessary

Pick up a bird guide (they should be hanging on a post in the aviary) and see how many different birds you can spot. Afterward, make a stop at the meerkat exhibit. Some people call it the "Timon exhibit" because he's a meerkat. (There are no Pumbaas here, though. Meerkats and warthogs don't get along in real life.)

Greetings, gorillas

At the end of the trail, you see families of gorillas. They are usually hanging out on the hills or playing. You might even spot a baby gorilla in the group. Szasha says, "Seeing the gorillas up close is amazing."

Disney's Animal Kingdom

Who am I?

- My uncle is a jerk
- My name means "lion" in Swahili
- I just can't wait to be king!

Answer: Simba

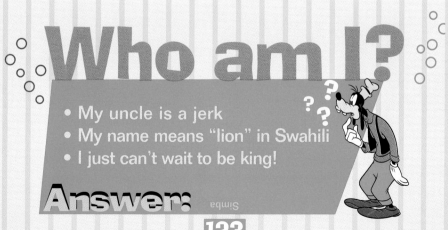

Conservation Station is a great place to stay dry when it rains.

♥HIDDEN MICKEY ALERT! There are Mickeys hiding all over the colorful mural at the entrance to the main building! Look for them in the eyes of the animals and on the wings of the butterflies.

Conservation Station

There's only one way to get to Conservation Station: on a train called the Wildlife Express. You can hop aboard in Africa. During the ride you get a behind-the-scenes look at the buildings where animals from the Safari are cared for.

Lend a helping hand

The exhibits at Conservation Station teach you what animals need to survive—and what people can do to help. There is an animal hospital, places for baby animals to sleep and get special care, and lots of shows meant to get you excited about conservation. There are even ways to find out about conservation projects near your home.

Talk to the animals

Many of the exhibits are interactive. In Song of the Rain Forest, you're surrounded by the sounds you might hear in a real rain forest. At the Look-in Lab, you can watch veterinarians care for baby animals. People can walk among animals like goats and sheep in The Affection Section. Go ahead and pet them, but remember: There's no feeding allowed.

Everybody has a favorite exhibit here. "Really young kids might like to pet the animals, but I like Song of the Rain Forest best," Eric says.

Kids care

The kids feel that Conservation Station is an important part of the park. "I'm glad there's a conservation area so we can learn to save the animals," Danielle T. says. Szasha agrees. "If we don't help them, they could become extinct," she adds.

Animal Cracker

Walt Disney loved animals. That's why they star in so many Disney movies. But sometimes it can be hard to keep all of the animated animals straight.

The character names in the left column are all mixed up. First see if you can unscramble them. Then match each name to the character's species in the right column.

1. NTOIM
2. ABBIM
3. OTANRT
4. LOAOB
5. AALK
6. TATA
7. PATRM
8. GOIA
9. ZANBAI
10. MIHELHIC

A. ELEPHANT
B. ANT
C. BEAR
D. BIRD
E. DOG
F. CATERPILLAR
G. GORILLA
H. MEERKAT
I. DEER
J. HYENA

How many of these animals can you spot in real life at Disney's Animal Kingdom?

ANSWERS: (1) Timon, H; (2) Bambi, I; (3) Tantor, A; (4) Baloo, C; (5) Kala, G; (6) Atta, B; (7) Tramp, E; (8) Iago, D; (9) Banzai, J; (10) Heimlich, F

Disney's Animal Kingdom

Asia is the largest continent on earth. It's almost twice as big as North America! The land called Asia in Animal Kingdom is a lot smaller than the real thing, but it gives you an idea of what the Asian continent is like. It has jungles and rain forests and magnificent animals. It's also home to the fastest raging river in Animal Kingdom. If you want to get wet, you can shoot the rapids down the river on a ride called Kali River Rapids. For a calmer experience, head for the Caravan Stage.

Maharajah Jungle Trek

Put on your walking shoes and keep your eyes peeled. This jungle trail is the place to spot strange, scaly animals called Komodo dragons, deer, gibbons (small apes that live in trees), giant bats, and lots of tigers. You'll also see many colorful birds along the way and tons of plants and trees. After all, it is a jungle.

You see the bats about halfway through your walk. Their wings are enormous! In some places, there's no glass between you and the bats. But don't worry—they're not interested in humans. Still, the kids agree that the bats can be a little creepy to look at. If you don't like bats, take Grace's advice: "Go when the sun is out. The bats are nocturnal, so they're not very active during the day."

♥**HIDDEN MICKEY ALERT!** The mural by t[h]e tigers is where this Mickey head is hidin[g]

Kali River Rapids

This is one of the wettest and wildest rides in Walt Disney World. Don't bother trying to pick a dry seat on the raft, because everyone gets wet! It begins as a peaceful raft trip through a rain forest. But things don't stay calm for very long. The raft bumps along down the river, spinning and turning every time it hits a rock. Along the way you catch a glimpse at how logging (cutting down trees for lumber) can destroy the rain forest. Don't be scared if you see a fire raging out of control—that's just part of the ride. You avoid the burning logs, but will you be safe from the waterfall? We won't tell. (You might want to bring a towel, just in case!)

You must be at least 42 inches tall to ride the rapids.

Disney's Animal Kingdom

Flights of Wonder

Live birds are the stars of this show that takes place on the Caravan Stage. They swoop and soar and do amazing tricks.

Sometimes one of the performers is a parrot named Groucho. He loves to entertain the audience. What is his special talent? He can sing! One of his favorite tunes is "How Much Is That Doggie in the Window?" Do you know the words to that song?

Camp Minnie-Mickey

Disney characters have their very own vacation spot right here in Animal Kingdom. It's called Camp Minnie-Mickey and it's a great place to meet Mickey, Minnie, Goofy, Pooh, Tigger, King Louie, Rafiki, and their friends. To find your favorite characters, just follow the trails through the forest. But save time to see the two shows while you're here.

Pocahontas and Her Forest Friends

Who can save the forest? The wise old tree, Grandmother Willow, knows the answer. But she won't tell. She wants Pocahontas to figure it out for herself.

This show is performed at Grandmother Willow's Grove. It takes you and Pocahontas on a journey through the forest. Together, you'll meet many different animals: an armadillo, a hawk, a skunk, even a boa constrictor. And they are all real! During the show, you will learn that every animal has its own special talent. You'll also discover which animal can stop the forest from being destroyed.

Festival of the Lion King

This is one spectacular musical show. Even if you have the movie memorized, you're in for a few surprises. All of the major characters from the movie are here, but they look a little different. Most of them are played by humans dressed in African costumes.

An action-packed performance

The theater has big stages that look like parade floats. (That's because they were once used in a parade at Disneyland!) On one, Simba sits atop Pride Rock. The wisecracking Pumbaa sits on another. Gymnasts dressed like monkeys use the center stage as a trampoline. They jump and do tricks.

Kids love the festival

"It's a terrific stunt show," David G. says. Grace agrees. "The songs and characters are wonderful," she adds. Jennifer thinks "the whole show is great, but the monkeys are the best part!" Eric loves it too, but he warns: "Expect some loud noises and flames that burst up suddenly."

This is a very popular show. Check a park guidemap for times and arrive at least 30 minutes before it starts.

Disney's Animal Kingdom

Entertainment

Don't be surprised if the performers at Animal Kingdom come right up to you—some walk on two legs, while others walk on four (or eight!). There are street musicians, storytellers, live animals, and many other things to entertain you along the way. Read all about them below.

AFRICAN ENTERTAINMENT

African music fills the air in the village of Harambe. Live bands perform here throughout the day.

ANIMAL ENCOUNTERS

Get to know our smaller animal friends as they roam through the park with their human keepers.

DINOLAND U.S.A. ENTERTAINMENT

A bunch of wacky performers is on the loose—and they will do anything to make you dig them! They usually drive around the area in a car, stopping to make noise along the way.

SAFARI VILLAGE ENTERTAINMENT

In this land storytellers tell animal tales, while music based on sounds of nature plays in the background.

Keep an eye out for performers dressed as colorful creatures big and small, from tigers to termites. These characters are called ARTimals because they look like artistic versions of the real animals. (They also look a little bit like animals from another planet.) They dance around and talk to the guests.

Where to Find Characters at Animal Kingdom

It's easy to find Disney characters at Animal Kingdom—they have a land all their own. **Camp Minnie-Mickey** is the best place to meet characters in this park. Different characters hang out at them all day. You might see Mickey, Goofy, Timon, Winnie the Pooh, Tigger, or other Disney favorites. Ask them to autograph page 160 of this book.

Flik, Francis, and Princess Atta can be found by the Tree of Life in **Safari Village**. Look for them when you leave It's Tough to be a Bug!

Donald Duck, Pluto, and other characters host breakfast at **Restaurantosaurus**.

ANIMAL KINGDOM TIPS

Animal Kingdom can get very hot, especially in the summer months. Head for Kali River Rapids or Conservation Station to cool off. And drink lots of water!

Go to the thrill rides—Countdown to Extinction and Kali River Rapids—early, before they get too crowded.

On the Kilimanjaro Safaris ride, look at the back of the seat in front of you. The pictures will show you which animals you're about to see.

Check the Tip Boards in Safari Village to find out how long the wait is for the most popular attractions.

It doesn't really matter what time you go on the safari—the animals are there all day long.

It's Tough to be a Bug! (inside The Tree of Life) is **very scary** to some kids. In it, bugs shoot quills, spiders fall from above, and creepy critters scamper beneath your seat.

It's fun to see how many animals you can find carved into The Tree of Life and the other buildings in Safari Village.

Look for your favorite Disney characters in Camp Minnie-Mickey. It's the best place to find them in the park.

Can't find your parents? Ask the closest Disney cast member for help.

Check out the thunder and lightning effects inside the Rainforest Cafe.

Attraction Ratings

COOL
(Check It Out)

- The Oasis
- Flights of Wonder
- Cretaceous Trail
- Radio Disney River Cruise
- Conservation Station

REALLY COOL
(Don't Miss)

- Tarzan Rocks!
- The Boneyard Playground
- Maharajah Jungle Trek
- Pocahontas and Her Forest Friends
- 2000 Dinosaur Jubilee

THE COOLEST
(See at Least Twice)

- Kilimanjaro Safaris
- Kali River Rapids
- Festival of the Lion King
- Countdown to Extinction
- It's Tough to be a Bug!
- Pangani Forest Exploration Trail

Your favorite Animal Kingdom attractions

Everything Else in the World

No matter what you're interested in—water fun, sports, or animals—Walt Disney World has enough to make every minute of your vacation a blast. After you visit the theme parks, there's still so much to do. There are three water parks, speedy boats to rent, horses to ride, a gigantic arcade, and lots of neat shopping spots.

If you're into sports, check out Disney's Wide World of Sports complex, rent a bike, or test your skills at miniature golf. For a peek at some Disney secrets, take a behind-the-scenes tour.

In this chapter, you can read up on all the extra activities and find out about hotels and restaurants at Walt Disney World. Then you can help your family decide where to stay, where to eat, and what to do when you're not at the theme parks.

Disney Diary

Goofy things are always happening at Walt Disney World. Fill in the blanks below (you can ask a friend, or do it yourself) with the type of word that is missing—a noun, adjective, verb, number, or name. Then read the finished sentences to find out what you've been telling your diary about Walt Disney World.

When I first got to Walt Disney World I was so __impressed__ (adjective)! There was so much to see and __do__ (verb). Where to begin? I started by riding __Safaris__ (ride name). Wow, that was the most __natural__ (adjective) ride I've ever been on. It made me __smile__ (verb) the whole time!

Afterward, I saw __Chip Eeyore__ (Disney character) and __Dale Pooh__ (Disney character). There were lots of __people__ (plural noun) asking for their autographs, so I had to __shout__ (verb) and __wave__ (verb) to get their attention. I asked them to sign my __book__ (noun).

I saw at least __10__ (number) characters during my trip. The biggest surprise was when I heard Cinderella singing by her wishing __fountain__ (noun). Her voice sounded so __soft__ (adjective). Everybody in Fantasyland stopped to __listen__ (verb) when they heard it!

But the best part was when I saw Aladdin __flying__ (verb) on a magic __carpet__ (noun). I told him I was going to miss Walt Disney World when my trip was over. "Here's something to remember us by," he said, and handed me a _____ (adjective) _____ (noun).

That's one vacation I won't forget for __100000__ (big number) years!

Waters of the World

It's easy to get wet, stay cool, and have fun at Walt Disney World. That's because it's a water wonderland. Choose from three water parks or take a dip in your hotel pool. If you're under the age of 10, you must bring a grown-up with you to the water parks.

Typhoon Lagoon

A typhoon is a powerful, windy storm. It dumps huge amounts of rain and sends objects flying through the air. This water park looks like a typhoon hit it. There's even a boat stuck on a mountain top! Of course, a storm didn't really put the boat there— Disney Imagineers did. They also put in pools, water slides, and a raft ride.

Catch a wave

The biggest pool here is like a small ocean. It has 5-foot waves. That makes body-surfing fun. There are also three speed slides to try. They send you zipping through a dark cave. For a calmer ride, you can slip into a tube and float along a river. Afterward, you can glide down more water slides.

There's also a special area just for younger kids—Ketchakiddee Creek. It has small slides and other games.

Swim with the sharks

Shark Reef is an amazing part of Typhoon Lagoon. It's the home of nurse sharks, bonnethead sharks, and leopard sharks. And you can splash around with them. Don't worry—these sharks are friendly. They don't mind when people swim in their tank. Are you brave enough to swim with the sharks? (You must be at least 10 years old.)

HOT TIP

Ready for a challenge?
Take the rock-climbing
trip offered at
Blizzard Beach.

Everything Else in the World

Blizzard Beach

Would you wear a bathing suit to a snow-covered mountain? Probably not. But you should wear one to Blizzard Beach. It looks like a place to ski, but it's really a water park. So don't worry if you can't ski. Nobody skis down the mountain here. They slide!

Reach the peak

Like a real ski resort, all the action centers around a mountain. In this case, it's Mount Gushmore. To get to the top, you can take a chair lift. The ride gives you a fantastic view of the whole park.

The scariest slide on the mountain is Summit Plummet. It begins 120 feet in the air, on a platform that looks like a ski jump. It drops you down a steep slide at about 60 miles per hour. That's faster than many cars go on the highway.

Slip-sliding away

There are plenty of other ways to slide down the mountain. Tube slides, body slides, and inner-tube rides can keep you busy all day long. It's fun to body-surf in the wave pool, too.

For preteens, there's Ski Patrol Training Camp, with its "iceberg" obstacle course, and ropes for swinging into the water. Tike's Peak is a special place for younger kids. It has slides and a snow-castle fountain play area.

As Karyn says, "This is one awesome water park."

Bring water shoes
to the water parks.
The ground gets hot—
and so do your feet!

Everything Else in the World

River Country

This may be the smallest Disney water park, but you can still have big fun here. You can zip down water slides, shoot the rapids in a tube, and swing from a rope and then drop into the lake. *Kerplunk!*

Disney Imagineers got the idea for River Country from books by Mark Twain: *The Adventures of Tom Sawyer* and *The Adventures of Huckleberry Finn.* In both stories, the boys splash in their favorite swimming spot.

Tom and Huck don't visit River Country—but other characters sometimes do. Goofy, Chip, and Dale are here to celebrate the Fourth of July all summer long. You can meet them, play tug-of-war, and join in potato sack races during the All-American Water Party. You might even get picked to be in a special parade!

To find out when the party is happening, ask a parent to call 407-939-4636.

Let's Get Wet!

Many other places around Walt Disney World offer chances to get wet. At the Magic Kingdom, head for Splash Mountain and sit on the right side of the log. Or hang around Donald's Boat at Mickey's Toontown Fair. Ariel's Grotto also has squirting water to play in. At Epcot, go to Ice Station Cool by Innoventions. Or play in the mist at the Cool Wash outside of Test Track in Future World. At the Disney-MGM Studios, there is a fire hydrant on New York Street that squirts water. Nobody stays dry at Kali River Rapids in Disney's Animal Kingdom. There are squirting fountains at the Downtown Disney Marketplace, too.

Fort Wilderness

Fort Wilderness is tucked away in a wooded area of Walt Disney World. (It isn't really a fort. It's a campground.) You can stay overnight or just come for a day. There are tennis and volleyball courts, and a marina with lots of boats. River Country, described on page 138, is also nearby. You could spend days here and not run out of things to do. If you only have a couple of hours, explore the petting farm and rent a boat for a ride around Bay Lake.

Petting Farm

Chickens, goats, pigs, and sheep live on a small farm at Fort Wilderness. Some of the animals like people to pet them. Others enjoy eating pellets from kids' hands (you can buy their special food from a dispenser that looks like a gumball machine).

Most kids think the farm is fun. "You can get close to the animals without being afraid," says Lissy. Karyn says, "If you really like animals, you'll have fun no matter how old you are."

More Fort Wilderness Fun

Fort Wilderness offers lots of other things to do. You can rent a canoe for a trip along the campground's canals. Or you can rent a bicycle and explore one of the many trails. At the Tri-Circle-D Ranch, you can see the champion horses that pull the trolleys in the Magic Kingdom. (They live in a barn near Pioneer Hall.)

Kids over 9 years old can take a trail ride on horseback. You can also enjoy a Fort Wilderness hayride, go fishing, or rent a speedboat.

Sports

Kids who like sports can find plenty of ways to keep active at Walt Disney World. You can rent bikes or boats at one of the resorts, or play miniature golf on one of Disney's themed courses. To see athletes at work, visit Disney's Wide World of Sports complex. Read on to find out how.

Disney's Wide World of Sports Complex

Sports fans should plan a visit to this exciting complex. It has facilities for every sport you can imagine. The Atlanta Braves baseball team comes here for spring training. The Harlem Globetrotters basketball team and the Orlando Rays baseball team train and play here, too. (The O-Rays are a minor league team for the Tampa Bay Devil Rays.)

Watch a game

You can spend a day watching lots of amateur events. Tickets cost $6.75 for kids ages 3 through 9, and $8 for anyone 10 or older. If you want to see a professional game, you have to buy your tickets ahead of time. The prices vary. Have a parent call 407-363-6600 for information.

Play ball

Do you like to play football? If so, the NFL Experience activity area is perfect for you. There are places to practice running, passing, punting, and catching—just like the pros do! (It's on an outdoor field at the sports complex.)

Water Mouse Boats

A Water Mouse is a speedy little boat that you can rent. And it delivers big thrills. If you are 12 or older, you can drive one all by yourself.

A Water Mouse ride gets very high marks from kids. "It's awesome," says Brian L. "I was turning into the waves and one splashed on top of me." David B. thinks it's neat to drive your own boat. "This is fun that you definitely can't miss," he says.

You can rent a Water Mouse boat at many Disney resorts. The cost is about $18 for a half hour.

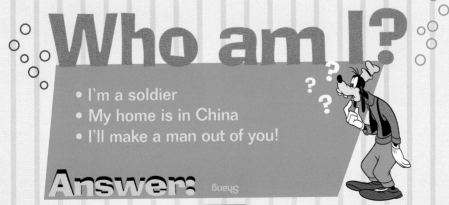

Who am I?

- I'm a soldier
- My home is in China
- I'll make a man out of you!

Answer: Shang

Miniature Golf

Even if you've never held a golf club before, you'll probably enjoy mini golf. It's fun to play, and full of surprises.

Fantasia Gardens

If you have seen the movie *Fantasia*, you'll know how this miniature golf course got its name. Where else will you find hippos on tiptoe, dancing mushrooms, or xylophone stairs?

The holes are grouped by musical themes. At the Dance of the Hours hole, watch the hippo standing on an alligator. If you hit the ball through the gator's mouth, the hippo dances!

The cost is $7.50 to play one round for kids ages 3 through 9, and $9.25 for anyone 10 or older.

Disney's Winter Summerland

Sometimes even Santa Claus needs a vacation. Just like you, he picked Walt Disney World as the perfect place to go and have fun.

As the story goes, Santa and his helpers built these mini-golf courses as a place to relax and enjoy the sun. That's why one looks like a beach, with sandcastles and surfboards on it. But then the elves got homesick, so they built a second course that reminded them of the North Pole. Everything looks like it's covered in snow! There are even igloos and snowmen, and holes for ice fishing.

For a bit of a challenge, try the summer course. It's a little harder than the winter course. Santa is snoozing at one of the trickiest holes. You have to hit the ball across his lap without waking him up. The winter holes offer fun surprises, too. Get the ball in one of the holes and Mickey himself pops out of the present!

The cost is $7.50 to play on one course for kids ages 3 through 9, and $9.25 for anyone 10 or older.

Camp Disney

Disney Imagineers would make great magicians. They use tricks all the time to create special effects for attractions at Walt Disney World. Like at Voyage of The Little Mermaid when bubbles float up into the audience. It might not seem like blowing bubbles requires much magic. But it's getting them to float *up*, and not fall *down*, that's the tricky part. How do they do it? That's one of the Imagineers' best secrets. (But here's a hint: The trick wouldn't work without the help of helium.)

Can you keep a secret?

The Imagineers are very good at keeping secrets. They don't like to share the secrets behind all of the tricks they use because that could spoil the illusion. But if you're really curious, there is one place to learn some good secrets. It's called Camp Disney, at the Disney Institute.

Many of the programs at Camp Disney are about entertainment. But some are about art or nature. One of them even teaches you how to rock climb. Depending on which class you take, you might go on a behind-the-scenes tour of the Disney-MGM Studios, make your own comic strip, or create a sculpture.

So many choices

There are lots of programs to pick from, and new ones are always being added. They are popular, so be sure to plan ahead if you want to include one in your vacation. You might even be able to get school credit for some of them.

A half-day program costs $69 and a full-day program is $99. You must be at least 7 years old to participate. For more information, have a parent call 800-496-6337. The Disney Institute offers many programs for grown-ups, too—so your parents won't feel left out!

Downtown Disney

♥HIDDEN MICKEY ALERT! Some of the Marketplace's dancing water fountains form the shape of you know who!

What has interesting shops and restaurants, movies, dance spots, boats to rent, and much more? Downtown Disney! It has three different sections: the West Side, the Marketplace, and Pleasure Island.

The West Side

This is the newest section of Downtown Disney. It has places to shop, eat, and catch a movie, plus a huge arcade called DisneyQuest (read all about it on the next page).

There's even an exciting show by Cirque du Soleil (pronounced: *sirk due so-LAY*). It's performed in a building that looks like a giant circus tent—but this show's not like an ordinary circus! You won't see a Ring Master or wild animals. Instead, there are gymnasts and acrobats dressed in colorful costumes. They twist their bodies, and dance in unusual ways.

The Marketplace

Looking for that perfect souvenir? The best place to look is in the Marketplace. There are dozens of shops to browse in. You can also make a wacky creation at the Lego Imagination Center. As Kirsti says, "It's the coolest! You can build things. There are also life-size Lego models, like a painter, and a dinosaur. There's even a snoring man."

Amy's favorite place to shop is the World of Disney store. It's the biggest Disney store in the world.

Pleasure Island

You might think this place is just for grown-ups—but kids can have fun at Pleasure Island. Especially kids who like to dance. Kids can bring their parents to three clubs: the Wildhorse Saloon (country music), 8TRAX (1970s tunes), and Rock N Roll Beach Club (rock 'n' roll, of course).

If you don't dance, don't worry. There are also games to play, outdoor shows, and fireworks to watch every night. You can even get a temporary Mickey Mouse tattoo!

DisneyQuest

This is the biggest arcade in the World—Walt Disney World, that is! It's filled from top to bottom with every game imaginable. With all the beeps and buzzers in this place, it practically sounds like you are standing in one giant video game. Even the elevator has special effects!

Pick a zone

DisneyQuest is separated into four different areas called "zones." In the **Explore Zone** you can visit far away places on virtual reality adventures. You might take a magic carpet ride with Aladdin or ride the rapids on a prehistoric jungle cruise.

The center of the **Score Zone** is a gigantic pinball game called Mighty Ducks Pinball Slam. In it, the people are giant joysticks! This zone is also the place to find all different kinds of brand-new video games.

Future Imagineers will love the **Create Zone**. Here you can take a short animation class, try computer painting, or have stickers made out of your photo. You can also design your own roller coaster and then ride it on CyberSpace Mountain, a virtual reality ride that goes upside down and twists all around.

In the **Replay Zone** you get prizes for the points you earn on some of

the games. Choose from favorites like Skee Ball and Whack an Alien (it's the *Toy Story* version of Whack a Mole). There's also a room full of video games that were popular more than ten years ago. Ask your parents if they remember them.

Take a break

There is so much to choose from! The kids all agree that you could spend all day here. But it's also a good idea to take some breaks along the way. For a quick meal or a tasty dessert, stop by the Cheesecake Factory Express—it's inside Disney-Quest. "At some of the tables you can even surf the Internet while you eat," Eric says.

DisneyQuest costs $20 for kids ages 3 through 9, and $25 for anyone 10 or older. (Prices may change.)

Walt Disney World Resorts

There are 19 resorts on the Walt Disney World property. That means there are enough rooms at Walt Disney World for you to stay in a different spot every night for more than 60 years!

Just like the rides at the parks, each of the resorts has its own special theme. And all of the resorts are fun to stay at. But they are fun to visit, too. So if you have time, you might want to stop by some of them—to have a meal or just to enjoy the atmosphere.

Near the Magic Kingdom

CONTEMPORARY

This was the first Walt Disney World hotel. It looked very modern when it was built in 1971 (that's how it got its name). When it opened it had a talking elevator and a monorail station right in the middle of it. It still has these things today, plus a huge arcade and Chef Mickey's—one of the best character restaurants in Walt Disney World.

Contemporary Tip

In the center of the resort is a mural that's 90 feet tall. There are colorful pictures of children and animals all over it. One of the goats has 5 legs. See how long it takes you to spot him!

FORT WILDERNESS

Bring a camper or rent a cabin at this pretty wooded campground. This resort is full of activities. You can go for a hayride, visit the petting farm, or take a trip through the woods on a pony. At night, Chip and Dale come over to roast marshmallows by the campfire with the guests. This is also home to the popular dinner show called the Hoop-Dee-Doo Musical Revue.

Fort Wilderness Tip

There are lots of trees in the woods of Fort Wilderness. But there's only one that's famous. It's called the Lawn Mower Tree. You'll know why when you find it!

The Monorail

The monorail connects the Magic Kingdom with the **Contemporary**, **Polynesian**, and **Grand Floridian** resorts. It's also the best way to get from the Magic Kingdom to Epcot or the Transportation and Ticket Center. At some stations a family can sit up front, with the driver. Ask a cast member if you can take a turn.

GRAND FLORIDIAN

This elegant hotel looks like a huge mansion from the 1900s. At first, it seems to be designed for grown-ups, but it's also fun for kids. There are special activities, like face painting and storytelling. At night you can sit in a big, comfy chair and listen to an old-fashioned band play in the main building. There is also a pretty pool with roses all around it. The monorail stops here, too.

Grand Floridian Tip

All the guests staying at this resort are given a special robe to use during their visit. If you're staying here, ask a parent to request a child-size robe for you!

POLYNESIAN

The plants and trees at this hotel make it look like a tropical island. The live parrots and waterfalls in the main building make the setting seem real even when you're indoors. There's a pool that looks like it's part of a coral reef, and a beautiful beach with hammocks to rest on. The monorail also has a station here.

Polynesian Tip

Join the Big Kahuna in welcoming the night at the weekend torch-lighting ceremonies. Before the torches are lit, there is a terrific flame throwing act.

WILDERNESS LODGE

With its log columns and totem poles, this hotel looks like a national park from the American Northwest. The fireplaces and rocking chairs in the main building make you feel right at home. Outside there's an erupting geyser and a pool that looks like it's part of a hot spring. There are so many Hidden Mickeys here that there's even a tour and contest to see how many you can find!

Wilderness Lodge Tip

Look for the "Proterozoic Fossils and Minerals" display. It's a rock key to the strata of the giant Grand Canyon fireplace in the main lobby.

Near Epcot and the Disney-MGM Studios

BOARDWALK

This hotel is designed to look like Atlantic City, New Jersey, once did. Just like on an old-fashioned boardwalk, there are games and snack stands here for everyone to enjoy. You can rent a special bicycle built for four, or swim in a pool that looks like an amusement park.

BoardWalk Tip

Look for a crystal globe under a chandelier in the main building. It's actually a Disney time capsule that will be opened on Walt Disney World's 50th anniversary.

CARIBBEAN BEACH

This happy and colorful hotel looks like the islands of the Caribbean. You can have fun in the sun all day at its beaches and pools.

Caribbean Beach Tip

Don't worry about packing a sand bucket or shovel—the kids meals at the food court come with them!

DIXIE LANDINGS

The buildings at this hotel look like mansions and country homes from the Old South. The food court is designed after a cotton mill and it has a real working waterwheel that's 30 feet tall. Inside you can actually see the cotton being pressed.

Dixie Landings Tip

If you like to fish, head down to the Ol' Fishin' Hole. The resort has poles to rent and worms to buy.

OLD KEY WEST

The townhouses that make up this resort have all the comforts of home. Most rooms have VCRs, and movie rentals are available. The palm trees and sunny design make it a warm and welcoming place.

Old Key West Tip

Kids ages 5 through 10 can sign up for an Un-Birthday Party. You'll enjoy the games and the cupcake that comes with it.

PORT ORLEANS

The special details at this hotel make it look like the city it's named for—New Orleans, Louisiana. There's a long river, and a fun pool with a curving dragon slide.

Port Orleans Tip

The best way to get from this resort to Downtown Disney is on a boat—it's called the Sassagoula River Cruise. It also takes you to Dixie Landings, where guests staying at Port Orleans can use the pools and playground.

SWAN AND DOLPHIN

You can't miss the dolphin and swan statues that sit on top of these two hotels—they're gigantic. Together the hotels have lots to do and many restaurants to eat at. (One is a fun ice cream parlor called Dolphin Fountain.) You can walk to Epcot from both hotels.

Swan and Dolphin Tip

There are 250 swan and dolphin statues at this resort. Some are big, but some are very small. See how many you can spot.

THE VILLAS AT THE DISNEY INSTITUTE

There are several types of villas, including "treehouses" on thick stilts. Most of the people who stay here take Disney Institute classes. Sometimes special movies are shown or plays are performed for the resort's guests and visitors.

Disney Institute Tip

The Disney Institute has a whole set of programs designed just for kids. And you don't have to be staying at the resort to sign up for them. Read all about them on page 143.

YACHT AND BEACH CLUB

These two connected hotels are designed after the homes near the beaches of Massachusetts. Even the pool makes you feel like you're at the beach—the bottom of it is covered with real sand!

Yacht and Beach Club Tip

Be sure to bring your sneakers. One of the best parts about staying here is that you can walk from the hotel to Epcot or the BoardWalk.

READER TIP

"If you stay at a Disney hotel, make sure to ask for a wake-up call. It's usually Mickey or one of his friends."

Raquel (age 7)
Miami, FL

Near Animal Kingdom

ALL-STAR RESORTS

There are three All-Star resorts, and each of them has its own theme—sports, music, or movies. It's easy to tell which All-Star you're at, because they have giant icons that are even bigger than the buildings. At All-Star Music look for the big cowboy boots. A huge football helmet shows you you're at All-Star Sports. And when you see a 38-foot-tall Buzz Lightyear, there's no doubt you're at All-Star Movies.

All-Star Tip

There are many Hidden Mickeys to hunt for. Start your search at the main statues in each of the resorts.

CORONADO SPRINGS

The land at this hotel looks like parts of the Southwestern U.S. and Mexico. The buildings are the color of clay. There's a pool that looks like an ancient pyramid with a slide that passes under a spitting jaguar. Beside it is a sandbox with ancient treasures waiting to be uncovered.

Coronado Springs Tip

Some of the food at the restaurant here might be new to you. If you don't like Mexican food, be sure to order from the kid's menu.

Disney Cruise Line

Set sail on a Disney ship with Mickey and his friends. You visit Walt Disney World for a few days and then cruise to the Bahamas. Each ship has special activity areas, pools, and programs just for kids, so you can do your own thing while your parents relax. Szasha says, "There's a whole deck just for kids." Dan thinks "it's not like an ordinary cruise." Michael agrees. "It's fun and different," he says, "and something I haven't done before."

The kids think the best part is getting to explore Disney's private island. It's called Castaway Cay. Danielle T. says, "Castaway Cay is so cool! There are all sorts of interesting things you can do. I've always wanted to go snorkeling, and I can do that there!"

Restaurants

Eating at Walt Disney World can be as much fun as riding Splash Mountain (well, almost as much fun!). Here are our suggestions for the best spots for kids to eat in each theme park, and what to order there.

Magic Kingdom
Best Places for Kids to Eat

Aunt Polly's Dockside Inn . . . . Peanut butter and jelly sandwiches
Casey's Corner . . . . Hot dogs
Cinderella's Royal Table . . . . Macaroni and cheese
Cosmic Ray's Starlight Cafe . . . . Veggie burgers
Crystal Palace . . . . Chicken fingers
Fantasyland Pretzel Stand . . . . Cinnamon pretzels
Liberty Square Market . . . . Fruit
Lunching Pad at Rockettower Plaza . . . . Turkey legs
Main Street Bake Shop . . . . Chocolate chip cookies
Main Street Confectionery . . . . Candy and crispie treats
Pecos Bill Cafe . . . . Chili
Pinocchio Village Haus . . . . Hamburgers
Plaza Ice Cream Parlor . . . . Ice cream
Plaza Pavilion . . . . Pizza

Epcot
Best Places for Kids to Eat

Alfredo's (in Italy) . . . . Spaghetti
Cantina de San Angel (in Mexico) . . . . Nachos
Cheese and Pasta Stand (in The Land) . . . . Macaroni and cheese
Electric Umbrella (in Innoventions) . . . . Hot dogs
Kringla Bakeri og Kafe (in Norway) . . . . .Cookies
Liberty Inn (in The American Adventure) . . . . Hamburgers
Pasta Piazza Ristorante (in Innoventions) . . . . Pizza
Pure and Simple (in Wonders of Life) . . . . Fruit
Refreshment Port (near Canada) . . . . Ice cream
Sandwich Shop (in The Land) . . . . . . Peanut butter and jelly sandwiches
Sommerfest (in Germany) . . . . Soft pretzels
Süssigkeiten (in Germany) . . . . Gummy Bears
Trapper Bob's Beaver Tail Cart (in Canada) . . . . .Fried dough

Everything Else in the World

Disney-MGM Studios
Best Places for Kids to Eat

Animal Kingdom
Best Places for Kids to Eat

Snack Wagons

All around the theme parks are wagons that sell soft drinks and quick snacks. If you like ice cream, try the Mickey Mouse Ice Cream Bar. Most kids love it!

Eating with the Characters

Kids of all ages enjoy eating with the characters. It's one of the best ways to see your favorite Disney stars. They will come right up to your table to meet you. Bring a camera because the characters are also happy to pose for photos. And don't forget your pen so you can collect some autographs!

Each of the theme parks has at least one restaurant that invites the characters over. Many of the resorts have character meals, too. They are very popular, so no matter which restaurant your family chooses, it's a good idea to make priority seating arrangements ahead of time. Ask a parent to call 407-WDW-DINE (939-3463).

Character meals aren't just fun because you get to see the characters. They're special because the food is served in a special way. Depending on which restaurant you choose, the meal will either be presented in a buffet or family-style. Picky eaters may prefer one of the buffets—with so much to choose from, you're sure to find something you like!

Everything Else in the World

Dinner Shows

Hoop-Dee-Doo Musical Revue

Entertainers sing, dance, and tell jokes while you chow down on chicken, ribs, and corn. Danielle G. says, "They get everyone in on the fun and put on a wonderful show." David B. thinks it's "very funny. I was laughing the whole time," he says.

All-American Backyard Barbecue

Mickey's having a barbecue, and you are welcome to join the fun. You can eat all the hot dogs, barbecued ribs, and strawberry shortcake you want, while a live band plays country music. After dinner, there's a show for kids, games, and dancing with the Disney characters.

Polynesian Luau

Aloha! That means "hello" (and "goodbye") in Hawaiian. You'll hear it a lot at this show. Performers do the hula and other Hawaiian dances, while waiters serve Polynesian food and fruity drinks.

Wonderland Tea Party

It's tea time at 1900 Park Fare in the Grand Floridian resort. Some afternoons Alice and the Mad Hatter throw a lunch party just for kids. You can decorate cupcakes, sip tea, and listen to the story of *Alice in Wonderland,* told by Alice herself.

Reservations for all of these shows should be made before you arrive at Walt Disney World. Your parents can call 407-WDW-DINE (939-3463).

Magical Memories

**The fun doesn't have to end when your vacation does.
Use these pages to preserve your Disney memories.**

On our way to Walt Disney World, we traveled by:
[✓] car [✓] plane [ ] bus [✓] boat [ ] train [ ] spaceship

I arrived at Walt Disney World on: _05/19 00_
(month/day/year)

I stayed for _16_ days.

These are the people I traveled with: _Mum Dad_
Jonathan

The name of our hotel was: _____

My usual bedtime is _9_ o'clock.

During my trip the latest I went to bed was _11_ o'clock.

The earliest I woke up was _4.53 (am)_ o'clock.

My first day at WDW I went to: _Animal Kingdom_

The first ride I went on was: _Safari_

157

Tape a used WDW ticket here

The weather at Walt Disney World was:
[✓] sunny [ ] rainy [ ] windy [ ] chilly [ ] snowy

This attraction wasn't what I expected: Snow Whites Scary

It surprised me because it was: not scary

My favorite ride was: Big Thunder Mountain Railroad

I went on it _____ times.

My least favorite ride was: Snow White

I didn't like it because it was: boring/babyish

The scariest ride I went on was: Tower of Terror/rock 'n' roller coaster

If I were an Imagineer, this is the ride I would design: One like Dueling Dragons at Islands of Adventure

Tape a drawing of your favorite
Disney character here

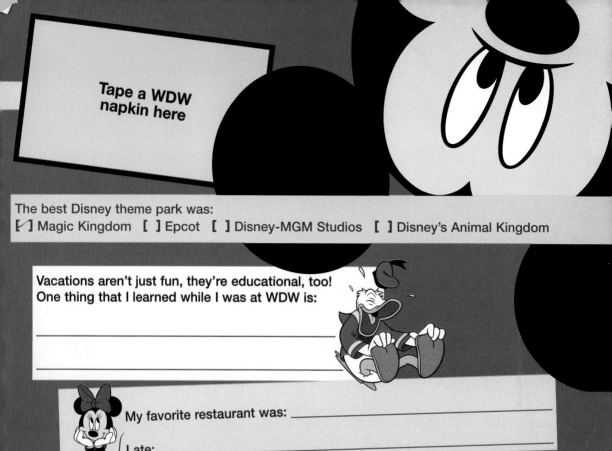

Tape a WDW napkin here

The best Disney theme park was:
[✓] Magic Kingdom [ ] Epcot [ ] Disney-MGM Studios [ ] Disney's Animal Kingdom

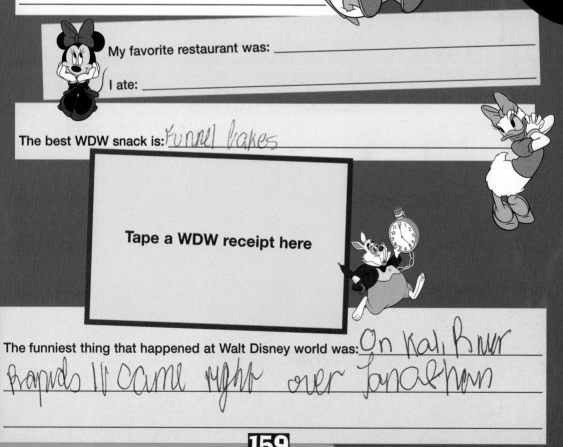

Vacations aren't just fun, they're educational, too!
One thing that I learned while I was at WDW is:

_____
_____

My favorite restaurant was: _____

I ate: _____

The best WDW snack is: Funnel Cakes _____

Tape a WDW receipt here

The funniest thing that happened at Walt Disney world was: On Kali River
Rapids it came right over Jonathan

Autographs

Disney characters love to give autographs.
Bring a pen and ask them to sign this page for you.